SpringerBriefs in Rights-Based Approaches to Social Work

AF711561

Series editor

More information about this series at http://www.springer.com/series/11694

Kathryn R. Libal · Scott Harding

Human Rights-Based Community Practice in the United States

Springer

Kathryn R. Libal
School of Social Work
University of Connecticut
West Hartford, CT
USA

Scott Harding
School of Social Work
University of Connecticut
West Hartford, CT
USA

ISSN 2195-9749 ISSN 2195-9757 (electronic)
ISBN 978-3-319-08209-7 ISBN 978-3-319-08210-3 (eBook)
DOI 10.1007/978-3-319-08210-3

Library of Congress Control Number: 2014950645

Springer Cham Heidelberg New York Dordrecht London

Springer is part of Springer Science+Business Media (www.springer.com)

Foreword

Even though you and I are in different boats, you in your boat and we in our canoe, we share the same River of Life.

—Chief Oren Lyons, Onandaga Nation, USA

The rights of every man are diminished when the rights of one man are threatened.

—John F. Kennedy, Civil Rights Announcement, June 11, 1963

For over a century, social workers have worked to improve the lives and situations of individuals, families, and communities. Social workers, often acting on behalf of the state's interests, typically intervened according to what they themselves perceived to be deficits in the lives and behaviors of persons in need. This approach to working with people patronizes, stigmatizes, and too often revictimizes those we seek to assist. It is long past time to revitalize and reframe our approach to working with those we seek to serve. The books in this series reframe deficit models used by social work practitioners and instead propose a human rights perspective. Rights-based social work shifts the focus from human needs to human rights and calls on social workers and the populations they work with to actively participate in decision-making processes of the state so that the state can better serve the interests of the population. The authors in the series share their strategies for empowering the populations and individuals we, as social workers, engage with as clinicians, community workers, researchers, and policy analysts.

The roots of social work in the United States can be traced to the pioneering efforts of upperclass men and women who established church-based and secular charitable organizations that sought to address the consequences of poverty, urbanization, and immigration. These were issues that were ignored by the public sphere at the time. Little in the way of training or methods was offered to those who volunteered their resources, efforts, and time in these charitable organizations until later in the nineteenth century when concepts derived from business and industry were applied to distribution of relief efforts in what became known as "scientific charity." This scientific approach led to the use of investigation, registration, and supervision of applicants for charity, and in 1877, the first American Charity

Organization Society (COS) was founded in Buffalo, New York. The popularity of the approach grew quickly across the country. COS leaders wanted to reform charity by including an agent's investigation of the case's "worthiness" before distributing aid because they believed that unregulated and unsupervised relief led to more calls for relief.

Around the same time, an alternative response to the impact of industrialization and immigration was introduced and tested by the settlement house movement. The first US settlement, the Neighborhood Guild in New York City, was established in 1886, and less than three years later, Jane Addams and Ellen Gates Starr founded Hull House in Chicago, which came to symbolize the settlement house movement in the United States. Unlike the individually oriented COS, the settlement house movement focused on the environmental causes of poverty, seeking economic and social reforms for the poor and providing largely immigrant and migrant populations with the skills needed to stake their claims in American society.

The settlement house movement spread rapidly in the United States and by 1910, there were more than 400 settlements (Trolander, 1987; Friedman & Friedman, 2006). Advocacy for rights and social justice became an important component of the settlement activities and led to the creation of national organizations like the National Consumers' League, Urban League, Women's Trade Union League, and the National Association for the Advancement of Colored People (NAACP). The leaders of the movement led major social movements of the period, including women's suffrage, peace, labor, civil rights, and temperance, and were instrumental in establishing a federal-level children's bureau in 1912, headed by Julia Lathrop from Hull House.

During this same period, the charity organization societies set to standardize the casework skills for their work with individuals. Their methods became a distinct area of practice and were formalized as a social work training program in 1898 known as the New York School of Philanthropy and eventually, the Columbia University School of Social Work. In 1908, the Chicago Commons offered a full curriculum through the Chicago School of Civics and Philanthropy (now the University of Chicago's School of Social Service Administration) based on the practices and principles of the settlement movement. By 1919, there were 17 schools of social work.

Efforts already underway to secure and strengthen pragmatically derived casework knowledge into a standardized format were accelerated following Abraham Flexner's provocative lecture in 1915 questioning whether social work was a profession because he believed it lacked specificity, technical skills, or specialized knowledge (Morris, 2008). By the 1920s, casework emerged as the dominant form of professional social work in the United States and remained primarily focused on aiding impoverished children and families but was rapidly expanding to work with veterans and middle-class individuals in child guidance clinics.

As social work branched out to other populations, it increasingly focused on refining clinical treatment modalities and over time clinical work too often stood apart from community work, advocacy, and social policy. Although social work education standards today require all students to be exposed to clinical and casework, community practice, advocacy, research and policy, most schools do not prioritize the integrated practice of these areas in the advanced year of social work education (Austin & Ezell, 2004; Knee & Folsom, 2012).

Despite the development of sophisticated methods for helping others, social work practice overly relies on charity and needs-based approaches. These approaches are built on the deficit model of practice in which professionals or individuals with greater means diagnose what is "needed" in a situation and the "treatment" or services required to yield the desired outcome that has been set by the profession or other persons of advantage. Judgments of need are based on professional research, practice wisdom, and theory steeped in values (Ife, 2012). These values, research, theories, and practices typically reflect the beliefs of the persons pronouncing judgment, not necessarily the values and theories of the person who is being judged. This has the effect of disempowering and diminishing control of one's own life while privileging professionals (Ife, 2012). In turn, this risks reinforcing passiveness and perpetuating the violation of rights among the marginalized populations we seek to empower and at best maintains the status quo in society.

Needs-based approaches typically arise from charitable intentions. In social welfare, charity-based efforts have led to the labeling of persons worthy and unworthy of assistance, attributing personal behaviors as the cause of marginalization, poverty, disease, and disenfranchisement, and restricted the types of aid available accordingly. Judgments are cast by elites regarding who is deserving and who is not based on criteria that serve to perpetuate existing social, economic, and political relationships in charity-based approaches. Needs-based approaches attempt to introduce greater objectivity into the process of selecting who is helped and how by using evidence to demonstrate need and introducing effective and efficient interventions to improve the lot of the needy and society as a whole. Yet the solutions of needs-based efforts like charity-based ones are laden with the values of professionals and the politically elite and do not necessarily reflect the values and choices of the persons who are the object of assistance. Needs-based approaches prioritize the achievement of professionally established goals over the process of developing the goals, and, too often, the failure of outcomes is attributed to personal attributes or behaviors of individuals or groups who receive assistance. For example, the type of services a person diagnosed with a mental disorder receives in a needs-based approach will be often decided by authorities or experts according to their determination of what is best for the person and is likely to assume that a person with a mental disorder is incapable of making choices or at least not "good" choices. Programmatic success would then be evaluated according to adherence to the treatment plan prescribed by the persons with authority in the situation and may omit consumers' objections or own assessments of well-being.

Unlike needs-based and charity-based approaches, a rights-based approach places equal value on process and outcome. In rights-based work, goals are temporary markers that are adjusted as people perpetually re-evaluate and understand rights in new ways calling for new approaches to social issues. For example, having nearly achieved universal access to primary education, a re-evaluation of the right to education might lead to a new goal to raise the quality of education or promote universal enrollment in secondary education among girls. Rights-based approaches are anchored in a normative framework that are based in a set of internationally agreed upon legal covenants and conventions, which in and of themselves can provide a different and potentially more powerful approach. A key aspect of this approach posits the right of all persons to participate in societal decision making, especially those persons or groups whom are affected by the decisions. For example, Article 12 of the United Nations Convention on the Rights of the Child (UNCRC) asserts that states "shall assure to the child who is capable of forming his or her own views the right to express those views freely in all matters affecting the child, the views of the child being given due weight in accordance with the age and maturity of the child" (UNCRC, 1989). Likewise, the preamble to the United Nations Convention on the Rights of Persons with Disabilities (UNCRPD) holds states responsible for "redressing the profound social disadvantage of persons with disabilities and (to) promote their participation in the civil, political, economic, social, and cultural spheres with equal opportunities" (UNCRPD, 2006).

A rights-based approach requires consideration of the universally recognized principles of human rights: the equality of each individual as a human being, the inherent dignity of each person and the rights to self-determination, peace and security. Respect for all human rights sets the foundation for all civil, political, social, and economic goals that seek to establish certain standards of well-being for all persons. Rights-based efforts remove the charity dimension by recognizing people not only as beneficiaries, but as active rights holders.

One of the areas of value added by the human rights approach is the emphasis it places on the *accountability* of policy makers and other actors whose actions have an impact on the rights of people. Unlike needs, rights imply duties, and duties demand accountability (UN OHCHR 2002: paragraph 23). Whereas needs may be met or satisfied, rights are realized and as such must be respected, protected, facilitated, and fulfilled. Human rights are indivisible and interdependent and unlike needs that can be ranked, all human rights are of equal importance. A central dynamic of a rights-based approach is thus about identifying root causes of social issues and empowering rights holders to understand and if possible claim their rights while duty bearers are enabled to meet their obligations. Under international law, the state is the principal duty bearer with respect to the human rights of the people living within its jurisdiction. However, the international community at large also has a responsibility to help realize universal human rights. Thus, monitoring and accountability procedures extend beyond states to global actors—such as the donor community, intergovernmental organizations, international non-governmental organizations (NGOs) and transnational corporations—whose actions bear upon the enjoyment of human rights in any country (UN OHCHR, 2002: paragraph 230).

Table 1 summarizes the differences between charity-, needs-, and rights-based approaches.

It can be argued that rights-based practice is not strikingly different from the way many social workers practice. For example, the strengths perspective that has

Table 1 Comparison of charity-, needs-, and rights-based approaches to social issues

	Charity-based	Needs-based	Rights-based
Goals	Assistance to deserving and disadvantaged individuals or populations to relieve immediate suffering	Fulfilling an identified deficit in individuals or community through additional resources for marginalized and disadvantaged groups	Realization of human rights that will lead to the equitable allocation of resources and power
Motivation	Religious or moral imperative of rich or endowed to help the less fortunate who are deserving of assistance	To help those deemed in need of help so as to promote well-being of societal members	Legal obligation to entitlements
Accountability	May be accountable to private organization	Generally accountable to those who identified the need and developed the intervention	Governments and global bodies such as the donor community, intergovernmental organizations, international NGOs, and transnational corporations
Process	Philanthropic with emphasis on donor	Expert identification of need, its dimensions, and strategy for meeting need within political negotiation. Affected population is the object of interventions	Political with a focus on participatory process in which individuals and groups are empowered to claim their rights
Power relationships	Preserves status quo	Largely maintain existing structure, change might be incremental	Must change
Target population of efforts	Individuals and populations worthy of assistance	Disadvantaged individuals or populations	All members of society with an emphasis on marginalized populations
Emphasis	On donor's benevolent actions	On meeting needs	On the realization of human rights
Interventions respond to	Immediate manifestation of problems	Symptomatic deficits and may address structural causes	Fundamental structural causes while providing alleviation from symptomatic manifestations

become a popular approach in social work practice since the 1990s focuses on strengths, abilities, and potential rather than problems, deficits, and pathologies (Chapin, 1995; Early & GlenMaye, 2000; Saleebey, 1992a) and "interventions are directed to the uniqueness, skills, interests, hopes, and desires of each consumer, rather than a categorical litany of deficits" (Kisthardt, 1992: 60–61). In the strengths-based approach, clients are usually seen as the experts on their own situation and professionals are understood as not necessarily having the "best vantage point from which to appreciate client strengths" (Saleebey, 1992b, p. 7). The focus is on "collaboration and partnership between social workers and clients" (Early & GlenMaye, 2000: 120).

The strengths perspective has provided a way for many social workers to engage themselves and the populations they work with in advocacy and empowerment that builds upon capabilities and more active processes of social change. Indeed, strengths-based and rights-based approaches build upon the strengths of individuals and communities and both involve a shift from a deficit approach to one that reinforces the potential of individuals and communities. Both approaches acknowledge the unique sets of strengths and challenges of individuals and communities and engage them as partners in developing and implementing interventions to improve well-being giving consideration to the complexities of environments. However, the strengths-based perspective falls short of empowering individuals to claim their rights within a universal, normative framework that goes beyond social work to cut across every professional discipline and applies to all human beings. Rights-based approaches tie social work practice into a global strategy that asserts universal entitlements as well as the accountability of governments and other actors who bear responsibility for furthering the realization of human rights.

The link between social work and human rights normative standards is an important one as history has repeatedly demonstrated. In many ways, social work has been moving toward these standards (Healy, 2008) but has yet to fully embrace it. Social work has been a contradictory and perplexing profession functioning both to help and also to control the disadvantaged. At times social workers have engaged in roles that have furthered oppression (Ife, 2012) and served as a "handmaiden" to those who seek to preserve the status quo (Abramovitz, 1998, p. 512). Social benefits can be used to integrate marginalized populations but also be used to privilege and exclude, particularly when a charity-based approach is utilized. When conditional, benefits can also be used as a way to modify behaviors and as a means of collecting information on private individual and family matters.

This contradictory and perplexing role of social work is shown albeit, in an extreme case, by social work involvement in the social eugenics movement specifically promulgated by National Socialists leaders in the 1930s and 1940s (Johnson & Moorehead, 2011). Leading up to and during World War II, social workers were used as instruments to implement Nazi policies in Europe. Though the history of social work and social work education is different in each European country, in at least Germany, Austria, Switzerland, Czechoslovakia, and Hungary, authorities used social workers to exclude what the state considered at the time to be undesirable populations from assistance, to reward those who demonstrated loyalty and pledged to carry forth the ideology of the state, and to collect information on personal and family affairs for the state (Hauss & Schulte, 2009). University-based and other forms of social work training were closed down in Germany in 1933 when the National Socialists assumed control because welfare was regarded as superfluous and a "waste for persons useless to the national community" (*Volksgemeinschaft* as quoted in Hauss & Schulte, 2009, p. 9). "Inferiors" were denied support and social workers were re-educated in Nazi ideology to train mothers on how to raise children who were loyal and useful to the ambitions of the National Socialists (Kruse, 2009). Similarly in Hungary, where social workers were referred to as "social sisters," social workers were re-educated to train mothers about the value of their contributions to the state (mainly their reproductive capacity and rearing of strong children for the state) and were instrumental in the implementation of Hungary's major welfare program that rewarded "worthy" clients with the redistribution of assets from Jewish estates (Szikra, 2009). As Szrika notes, "In the 1930s social policy and social work constituted a central part of social and economic policy-making that was fueled by nationalist and anti-Semitic ideology, influenced by similar practices in Germany, Italy and Czechoslavakia" (p. 116). Following Nazi ideological inoculation based on eugenics and race hate, social workers in Austria were charged with the responsibility of collecting incriminating information regarding mental illness, venereal disease, prostitution, alcoholism, hereditary diseases, and disabilities that would then be used to deny social benefits, prohibit marriages, and even select children for Austria's euthanasia program (Melinz, 2009).

Using social workers to realize state ideology was also employed to advance the Soviet agenda beginning in 1918 (Iarskaia-Smirnova & Romanov, 2009). The provision of social services was distributed across multiple disciplines among the helping professions and the term social work was not used because of its association to Western social welfare (Iarskaia-Smirnova & Romanov, 2009). These professionals, often referred to as social agents (workers in nurseries and youth centers, activists in women's organizations and trade unions, nurses, educators and domestic affairs officials), were charged with the double-task of social care and control. Early on social agents contributed to the establishment of standards designating worthy and unworthy behavior and activities and practices such as censure and social exclusion designed to alienate those who did not comply with state goals (Iarskaia-Smirnova & Romanov, 2009).

The use of social workers to carry out goals seemingly in contradiction of social work's ethics can be found in many examples in the United States as well (Abramovitz, 1998). In his book, *The Child Savers: The Invention of Delinquency* (1965), Anthony Platt demonstrates that despite well-intentioned efforts to protect youth, the establishment of the juvenile justice system in the United States removed youth from the adult justice systems and in doing so created a class of delinquents who were judged without due process. Platt argues that "child savers should in no sense be considered libertarians or humanists" (Platt, 1965, p. 176). The juvenile justice system that these reformers—many of who were social work pioneers—created in the United States purposefully blurred the distinction between delinquent and dependent young people. Labeling dependent children as delinquents, most of whom had committed no crime, robbed them of their opportunity to due process. The state and various religious organizations were given open reign to define delinquency as they saw fit and children who were perceived to be out of order or young women who were viewed as immoral were committed to institutions or other forms of state supervision with no means of redress.

More recently, Bumiller's analysis of domestic violence in the United States rouses our consciousness of the ways in which social workers engaged with persons involved in domestic violence and/or rape may inadvertently squash rather than empower individuals and families (Bumiller, 2008). Bumiller (2008) uses sexual violence to demonstrate how lawyers, medical professionals, and social workers may be contributing to passivity of social service beneficiaries and in doing so, enlarge the state's ability to control the behaviors of its members. As Bumiller explains, our public branding of perpetrators of sexual violence as deserving of severe punishment and isolation allow us then to deem them incapable of rehabilitation, and so we offer few opportunities for perpetrators to rejoin society as functioning members. In contrast, we expend resources toward "treating" victims to turn them into successful survivors and in the process of doing so instill their dependency on the state. We do this by requiring victims who seek support and protection from the state to comply with authorities, which in many cases are social workers, and acquiesce to the invasion of state control into their lives. In return for protection and assistance, needy women and children often relinquish control of their own lives and are forced to become individuals who need constant oversight and regulation. "As women have become the subjects of a more expansive welfare state, social service agencies have viewed women and their needs in ways that have often discouraged them from resisting regulations and from being active participants in their own decisions" (Bumiller, 2008). Some social workers use professional authority to support a deficit approach that allows social workers to scrutinize the parenting skills, education, housing, relationships, and psychological coping skills of those who have experienced sexual violence and then prescribe behaviors necessary to access to benefits. Those who voice complaints and resist scrutiny may be denied benefits such as disqualifying women from TANF benefits who fail to comply with work requirements or cutting off assistance to women who return to violent relationships. As key actors in this process, social workers have the opportunity to legitimize women's voice both within social welfare institutions and within the confines of relationships rather than reinforcing dependency and in some circumstances, revictimizing the individuals by making compliance a prerequisite for assistance.

The commonality of these examples lies in the omission of a normative frame that transcends national borders. The foundation of a rights-based approach is nested in universal legal guarantees to protect individuals and groups against the actions and omissions that interfere with fundamental freedoms, entitlements, and human dignity as first presented in the Universal Declaration of Human Rights (United Nations, 1948). International human rights law is based on a series of international conventions, covenants, and treaties ratified by states as well as other non-binding instruments such as declarations, guidelines, and principles. Taken together these inalienable, interdependent, interrelated, and indivisible human rights are owned by people everywhere and responsibility to respect, protect, and fulfill these rights is primarily the obligation of the state.

Bonding social work practice to these international legal instruments obligates social workers to look beyond their own government's responses to social issues, to empower the populations they work with to have their voice heard, and to recast the neglected sovereignty of marginalized individuals and communities. It moves social workers away from being agents of the state to being change agents in keeping with the founding vision of social work. It reunites the different methods of social work practice by obligating all social workers to reflect on how public policies affect the rights of individuals and communities as well as how individual actions affect the rights of others (see Table 2). A rights-based approach compels social workers to look beyond existing methods of helping that too often exist to justify state intervention without addressing the root causes of the situation. It calls upon social workers who often act as agents of the state to acknowledge and act on their responsibility as moral duty bearers who have the obligation to respect, protect, and fulfill the rights of rights holders.

Rights-based approaches in social work have gained international acceptance in the past two decades more so outside of the United States than within. Social workers in the United States are relatively new to human rights practice, in part because of longstanding resistance known as "American exceptionalism" which

Table 2 Rights-based approaches to social work practice at different levels of intervention

Individuals seeking assistance are not judged to be worthy or unworthy of assistance but rather are viewed as rights holders. Social workers assist others in claiming their rights and helping others understand how individual rights have been violated. Interventions offered are not patronizing or stigmatizing, rather methods provide assistance based on the dignity of and respect for all individuals. Example of individual-centered change: *Sexually trafficked persons are viewed as rights holders whose rights were violated rather than as criminals and are offered healing services and other benefits to restore their wholeness.*
Community/group/organization efforts are redirected away from proving that they deserve or need a resource toward learning about how they can claim their entitlements to resources. Social workers facilitate human rights education among group members including knowledge of human rights instruments, principles, and methods for accessing rights. Example of group-centered change: *Groups are offered opportunities to learn about their housing rights, the change process in their community and learn skills so that they can claim their right to participation in community decisionmaking.*
Society redirects its social policies and goals to facilitate the realization of human rights including addressing human needs. Macropracticing social workers affect the policy process and goals by expanding means for all members of a society to have their voices heard in the decision-making process. Example of society-centered change: *Persons with disabilities are able to participate in the policy-making process through the use of technology that allows them to participate in meetings from their homes.*

allows the United States to initiate and even demand compliance of human rights abroad while repeatedly rejecting the application of international standards for human rights in the United States (Hertel & Libal, 2011). Most Americans are knowledgeable about civil and political rights, yet far fewer are as familiar with economic, social, and cultural rights. Relatively limited engagement in this area by social workers also stems from the perception that human rights activism is best led and achieved by lawyers or elite policy advocates. The books in this series are written to facilitate rights-based approaches to social work practice both in the United States and around the world and recognize that exposure to human rights multilateral treaties and applications may vary depending on where the reader was educated or trained.

A rights-based approach brings a holistic perspective with regards to civil, political, social, economic, and cultural roles we hold as human beings and a more holistic understanding of well-being that goes beyond the meeting of material needs. Our understanding of human rights is always evolving, and our methods, practices, research, interventions, and processes should evolve as our understanding deepens. The purpose of this series is to assist social work practitioners, educators, and students toward operationalizing a new approach to social work practice that is grounded in human rights. It is hoped that the books will stimulate discussion and the introduction of new methods of practice around maximizing the potential of individuals, communities, and societies. The books, like social work, reflect the wide range of practice methods, social issues, and populations while specifically addressing an essential area of social work practice. By using current issues as examples of rights-based approaches, the books facilitate the ability of social workers familiar with human rights to apply rights-based approaches in their practice. Each book in the series calls on social work practitioners in clinical, community, research, or policy-making settings to be knowledgeable about the laws in their jurisdiction but to also look beyond and hold states accountable to the international human rights laws and framework.

Fordham University, New York, NY Shirley Gatenio Gabel

References

Abramovitz, M. (1998). Social work and social reform: An arena of struggle. *Social Work, 43*(6), 512–526.

Austin, M. J., & Ezell, M. (2004). Educating future social work administrators. *Administration in Social Work, 28*(1), 1–3.

Bumiller, K. (2008). *In an abusive state: How neoliberalism appropriated the feminist movement against sexual violence*. Durham: Duke University Press.

Chapin, R. (1995). Social policy development: The strengths perspective. *Social Work, 40*(4), 506–514.

Early, T., & GlenMaye, L. (2000). Valuing families: Social work practice with families from a strengths perspective. *Social Work, 45*(2), 118–130.

Friedman, M., & Friedman, B. (2006). *Settlement houses: Improving the welfare of America's immigrants*. New York: Rosen Publishing.

Hauss, G., & Schulte, D. (Eds.). (2009). *Amid social contradictions: Towards a history of social work in Europe*. Opladen, Farmington Hills, MI: Barbara Budrich Publishers.

Healy, L. M. (2008). Exploring the history of social work as a human rights profession. *International Social Work, 51*(6), 735–746.

Hertel, S. & Libal, K. (2011). *Human Rights in the United States: Beyond Exceptionalism*. Cambridge.

Iarskaia-Smirnova, E., & Romanov, P. (2009). Rhetoric and practice of modernisation: Soviet social policy (1917–1930). In G. Hauss & D. Schulte (Eds.), *Amid social contradictions: Towards a history of social work in Europe*. MI: Barbara Budrich Publishers.

Ife, J. (2012). *Human rights and social work: Towards rights-based practice*. Cambridge: Cambridge University Press.

Johnson, S., & Moorhead, B. (2011). Social eugenics practices with children in Hitler's Nazi Germany and the role of social work: Lessons for current practice. *Journal of Social Work Values and Ethics, 8*(1). http://www.jswve.org.

Kisthardt, W. (1992). A strengths model of case management: The principles and functions of a helping partnership with persons with persistent mental illness. In D. Saleebey (Ed.), *The strengths perspective in social work practice*. New York: Longman.

Knee, R. T., & Folsom, J. (2012). Bridging the crevasse between direct practice social work and management by increasing the transferability of core skills. *Administration in Social Work, 36*, 390–408.

Kruse, E. (2009). Toward a history of social work training Germany—discourses and struggle for power at the turning points. In G. Hauss & D. Schulte (Eds.), *Amid social contradictions: Towards a history of social work in Europe*. MI: Barbara Budrich Publishers.

Melinz, G. (2009). In the interest of children: Modes of intervention in family privacy in Austria (1914–1945). In G. Hauss & D. Schulte (Eds.), *Amid social contradictions: Towards a history of social work in Europe*. MI: Barbara Budrich Publishers.

Morris, P. M. (2008). Reinterpreting Abraham Flexner's speech, 'Is social work a profession?' Its meaning and influence on the field's early professional development. *Social Service Review, 82* (1), 29–60.

Platt, A. M. (1965). *The child savers: The invention of delinquency*. Chicago, IL: University of Chicago Press.

Saleebey, D. (1992a). Introduction: Beginnings of a strengths approach to practice. In D. Saleebey (Ed.), *The strengths perspective in social work practice*. New York: Longman.

Saleebey, D. (Ed.). (1992b). *The strengths perspective in social work practice*. New York: Longman.

Szikra, D. (2009). Social policy and anti-semitic exclusion before and during WW II in Hungary: The case of productive social policy. In G. Hauss & D. Schulte (Eds.), *Amid social contradictions: Towards a history of social work in Europe*. MI: Barbara Budrich Publishers.

Trolander, J. A. (1987). *Professionalism and social change: from the settlement house movement to neighborhood centers, 1886 to the present*. New York: Columbia University Press.

United Nations. (1948, December 9). *Convention on the prevention and punishment of genocide*. Retrieved from http://www.ohchr.org/EN/ProfessionalInterest/Pages/CrimeOfGenocide.aspx.

United Nations. (1989, November 20). *Convention on the rights of the child*. New York: United Nations. Retrieved from http://www2.ohchr.org/english/law/pdf/crc.pdf.

United Nations Office of the High Commissioner for Human Rights (UN OHCHR). (2002). Draft Guidelines for a Human Rights Approach to Poverty Reduction Strategies 2002.

United Nations. (2006, December 13). *Convention on the rights of persons with disabilities*. New York: United Nations. Retrieved from http://www2.ohchr.org/english/law/pdf/disabilitiesconvention.pdf.

Acknowledgments

We thank the series editor, Shirley Gatenio Gabel, for her guidance and support throughout the writing of this book. We thank the editorial team at Springer as well and are grateful to Jennifer Hadley for her efforts to coordinate the production of the book. We are also grateful to Karen D'Angelo, who read the text and offered valuable editorial insights. And, thanks are owed to the various faculty and graduate students active in the University of Connecticut's Human Rights Institute and Economic and Social Rights Group. Our numerous discussions spurred the idea for this text.

Contents

Chapter 1
Human Rights-Based Approaches to Community Practice in the United States: A Call to Action

Where, after all, do universal rights begin? In small places, close to home—so close and so small that they cannot be seen on any maps of the world. Yet they are the world of the individual person; the neighborhood he lives in; the school or college he attends; the factory, farm or office where he works. Such are the places where every man, woman, and child seeks equal justice, equal opportunity, equal dignity without discrimination. Unless these rights have meaning there, they have little meaning anywhere. Without concerned citizen action to uphold them close to home, we shall look in vain for progress in the larger world.

Eleanor Roosevelt, "The Great Question," remarks delivered at the United Nations in New York on March 27, 1958 (United Nations, n.d.).

Introduction

Eleanor Roosevelt's statement on human rights being realized "close to home" through everyday acts of involvement in community life has new meaning today. Community-based organizations and other civil society groups increasingly invoke human rights in campaigns to challenge social inequality and other forms of injustice. Rights-based approaches in social work have also been gaining currency in the past 20 years. Internationally, social work scholars and practitioners utilize a human rights framework to conduct policy analysis and political advocacy, community practice (Ife, 2012; Zaidalkilani, 2011), and clinical practice (Berthold, 2015; Reichert, 2011). Social workers in the United States are relatively new to the field of contemporary human rights practice. This is due in part because of long-standing resistance to understanding social justice issues as involving human rights claims, stemming from a legacy of "American exceptionalism" (Hertel & Libal, 2011). Relatively limited engagement in this area by social workers also stems from the perception that human rights mobilization is best achieved by lawyers or professional policy advocates (Reichert, 2006). In the past such efforts in the judicial

K.R. Libal and S. Harding, *Human Rights-Based Community Practice in the United States*, SpringerBriefs in Rights-Based Approaches to Social Work,
DOI 10.1007/978-3-319-08210-3_1

and policy realms have relied on a top-down approach to achieve formal legal change to comply with international human rights norms. Though important, this work has often failed to adequately consider the value of grassroots mobilization and specific community-based efforts to promote and realize human rights (Armaline, Glasberg, & Purkayastha, 2011; Ife & Fiske, 2006; Ife, 2008). In the past two decades, social workers in the United States have become increasingly knowledgeable about human rights principles and international norms (Healy, 2008; Steen & Mathieson, 2005). At the same time, public interest lawyers and human rights advocates have solicited community social workers and allies to develop campaigns "from the ground up" (see the work of the National Economic and Social Rights Initiative and the US Human Rights Network, Class Exercises and Additional Resources). As this movement has matured in the United States, local organizations have made claims for social inclusion and equality using the language of human rights. Jewell, Collins, Gargotto, and Dishon (2009) argue that in the context of community organizing with welfare recipients and low-wage workers "using a human rights framework can stimulate a debate that emphasizes our ethical and moral right to basic necessities" (p. 310). While social work has a rich history of community-level "macro" practice (Rothman, 2007; Rubin & Rubin, 2008), explicit connections between community practice and human rights have only recently emerged (Androff, 2012; Ife, 2008; Reisch, Ife, & Weil, 2012). This book is an effort to bring together two strands of professional work—community practice and human rights practice—that are congruent and necessary to address together in order to advance human rights and social justice goals in the United States.

This chapter outlines the value of using a rights-based, rather than a needs-based or charitable, approach by community practitioners to address social exclusion and inequality. As a form of practice a rights-based approach seeks to hold government —at multiple levels—accountable for ensuring that human rights are met for all members of society. We define the concept of human rights, noting the legacy of "American exceptionalism" within the global human rights system, particularly with respect to economic and social rights. We illustrate the foundation for a "right to community," underscoring core values of social inclusion, civic engagement, and deliberative democracy as crucial factors in human rights mobilization. The chapter also outlines the strength of a rights-based approach to community-level advocacy and efforts to organize campaigns at varied levels of governance (municipal, regional, state, and national). We suggest that a rights-based approach offers the possibility of more participation by a broader segment of community members on specific campaigns. Thus, such efforts have the potential to include actors lacking traditional political power. We compare the congruence of this framework with classic models of community organizing, which emphasize affected groups having a central role in identifying key concerns and defining solutions. Community engagement is also critical for *implementation* of laws and policies. Without community participation, therefore, specific human rights gains made in the legal and policy realm may not be realized.

Defining Human Rights

There are two dimensions to human rights, one that is rooted in international human rights law and practices, and another that is normative or moral in nature and may transcend any given legal norms (Ife & Fiske, 2006). Gaining competence in international human rights law for most social workers requires learning a new language. It implies a need to become familiar with how to access resources that provide insight into the specific norms and standards being developed by UN bodies and at regional and national levels. In the United States, lack of familiarity and knowledge by social workers and society at large with the meanings and practices of human rights stems from a sense of "American exceptionalism," a concept explained in more detail below.

In the United States, the human rights document familiar to most people is the Universal Declaration of Human Rights (UDHR), adopted by the United Nations General Assembly in 1948. Embodied in the UDHR and the United Nations Charter are the founding principles of a evolving understanding of rights that all humans share, including economic, social, cultural, political, and civil rights. Less well understood is the system of human rights treaties, guidelines, and processes of implementing and monitoring compliance of human rights that takes place both at the United Nations and by regional human rights systems such as the European Court of Human Rights or the Inter-American Court of Human Rights.

Contemporary understandings of what counts as human rights in the United States emphasize *civil and political rights*, including the right to life; to be free from torture and enslavement; to liberty and security of the person; recognition before the law; freedom of belief, thought, and expression; right to participate in politics and public life; freedom of association; right to marry; and the right to one's own language and community, particularly in countries with diverse ethnic, national, and religious groups. Underpinning these political and civil rights are the principles of non-discrimination and equality, regarded as fundamental within a human rights framework. Civil and political rights are consonant with core values expressed in the US Constitution and have been viewed as *the* human rights for which the federal government should be held accountable.

Less recognized in the United States has been the grouping of rights known as *social, economic, and cultural rights* (Albisa, 2011; Lewis, 2009; Ploch, 2011). The Universal Declaration of Human Rights (United Nations, 1948) defines the basis for economic and social rights in several key principles. Article 22 establishes a right to social security and the "economic, social, and cultural rights indispensable" for dignity and human development. Article 23 defines rights related to work. Article 25 establishes a right to an adequate standard of living, in order to secure food, clothing, housing and medical care and necessary social services for individuals and families. This article also entails that everyone has a right to social security for the unemployed, sick, disabled, widowed, or elderly (see Class Exercises and Additional Resources section). Article 26 defines a right to education. Finally, Article 27 articulates that everyone has "the right to freely participate in the cultural life of the community, to enjoy the arts and to share in scientific advancement and benefits." Each of these articles in the Universal Declaration of Human Rights has been further elaborated in the International Covenant on Economic, Social and Cultural Rights (ICESCR) (United Nations, 1966). The United States has failed to join the ICESCR, however, claiming that it already achieves these ideals through policies and laws that allow *equal opportunity* for its citizens to become educated, work, and secure their own housing and other "goods" (Alston, 2009). Thus, the federal government's position is one of denial of any obligation or responsibility of the government to respect, protect, and fulfill economic and social rights. Despite this view, human rights advocates, community organizers, and other professionals from law, public health, nursing, and social work have begun to use the standards established in the ICESCR and other human rights treaties addressing economic and social rights.

Yet defining economic and social rights and building support within social work to advocate for the realization of specific rights—to adequate housing, health care, or food, for example—has been challenging. While many US social workers recognize addressing *human needs* as a primary goal of the profession, explicit reframing of such "needs" as rights is an uneven practice (Healy, 2008; Reichert, 2011). For example, human rights is often treated as something to address largely in the international realm in the National Association of Social Workers' (2012) compendium of policy action statements, *Social Work Speaks*. The collection of NASW policy statements largely fails to engage human rights directly in other policy statements, despite human rights dimensions to most of the areas addressed by the volume.

This book seeks to underscore the consonance between human rights norms and practices and community practice in the United States, with a focus on some of the most pressing structural issues of social inequality: health care, housing, and food as human rights concerns. These are central concerns of community organizing. Reframed as human rights matters, many organizers argue that new concepts, tools and tactics for social mobilization and policy formulation and implementation can be developed.

Social work literature addressing social and economic rights has emerged over the past 20 years and there are now several different approaches to defining human rights that are helpful to recognize. Ife (2006) includes rights to life, food, water, shelter, clothing, health, and safety under *survival rights* and suggests that rights to a basic standard of living, work, and social security are *economic rights*. He claims the right to family life, privacy, education, and choice of partner and sexuality are *social rights*. Hertel and Minkler (2007), experts in political science and economics, define *economic rights* as a right to an adequate standard of living, including rights to health and education; right to employment without discrimination; and a right to social security. In yet another permutation, Mishra (2005) categorizes adequate standard of living, adequate housing, food, access to health care, and social protection/social security as *social rights*. For our purposes, we address economic and social rights as entwined and do not separate the two terms "economic" and "social." We retain a focus on "economic and social rights" (rather than "survival rights") because of the widespread use of this framing in many fields, including social work, public health, social development, and law.

Since the adoption of the UDHR in 1948, governments, including the United States, and non-governmental actors have sought to define the parameters of human rights and mechanisms for securing them both within and between nation-states. In the 1940s, Americans such as Eleanor Roosevelt were deeply involved in processes to define human rights and develop methods for state enforcement (Glendon, 2002). Because of the advent of the Cold War and the rise of post-colonial movements, it took nearly 20 years for the Commission on Human Rights to craft two separate covenants which further elaborated and gave force to principles contained in the Universal Declaration (Nowak, 2005). The ICESCR and the International Covenant on Civil and Political Rights (ICCPR) were adopted by the United Nations in 1966 and came into force in 1976, after enough countries had ratified, or agreed to be bound by these treaties. These covenants, along with the UDHR are also known as the International Bill of Rights (Healy, 2008; Pollack & Rosman, 2012).

Other human rights treaties have been created since the founding of the United Nations and are monitored under the auspices of the Office of the High Commissioner for Human Rights. These include the International Convention on the Elimination of All Forms of Racial Discrimination (CERD) (United Nations, 1965); the Convention on the Elimination of All Forms of Discrimination Against Women (United Nations, 1979); the Convention Against Torture and Other Cruel, Inhuman, or Degrading Treatment or Punishment (United Nations, 1984); the Convention on the Rights of the Child (United Nations, 1989); the International Convention on the Protection of the Rights of All Migrant Workers and Members of Their Families (1990); the Convention on the Rights of Persons With Disabilities (United Nations, 2006); and the International Convention for the Protection of All Persons from Enforced Disappearance (United Nations, 2006). Additional human rights monitoring processes have developed in recent years at the United Nations through the Human Rights Council's Universal Periodic Review process and through special investigations by "rapporteurs" on wide-ranging topics, such as extreme poverty, violence against women, housing, and food.

Additional UN treaties address key human rights concerns, including a robust system monitoring labor rights by the International Labour Organisation, the lead agency for monitoring labor rights; the Convention on the Prevention and Punishment of Genocide (United Nations, 1948); and the Convention and Protocol Relating to the Status of Refugees (United Nations, 1951, 1967), administered by the United Nations High Commissioner for Refugees. At a regional level, the European Court of Human Rights and the Inter-American Commission of Human Rights, as well as the Inter-American Court of Human Rights, are also rich sources for human rights implementation or organizing, highlighting how human rights claims are adjudicated in other countries. The United States is a member of the Organization of American States and thus is subject to the jurisdiction of the Inter-American Commission to consider violations of the American Declaration of the Rights and Duties of Man (Inter-American Commission on Human Rights, 1948). But, the United States has not ratified the American Convention on Human Rights (Organization of American States, 1969) and is not subject to the authority of the Inter-American Court of Human Rights.

The Political Nature of Claiming Human Rights

Mobilization for human rights is an inherently political activity. As Michael Goodhart (2009) observes, "To assert a human right is to make a fundamentally political claim: that one is entitled to equal moral respect and to the social status, support, and protection necessary to achieve that respect … Yet human rights are not simply equivalent with human dignity or justice; they represent a certain kind of dignity or justice, one incompatible with subordination" (p. 4). Deka (2012) underscores this *political* aspect of human rights advocacy. He asserts that rights-based approaches to addressing poverty and social and economic rights realization are "based on a shift from a technical understanding of rights to a politically motivated understanding which is premised on three key components: that individuals have rights, the state or government is obliged to safeguard those rights, and people need to participate for the attainment of those rights" (Deka, 2012, p. 473).

Human rights practice is carried out locally, nationally, and internationally; while standards are set at regional and international levels, achieving gains to realize human rights and social justice requires consciousness-raising and social mobilization at the *local* level. Thus, while countries that agree to be bound by particular human rights treaties commit to respecting, protecting, and fulfilling specific rights, these obligations are usually not fulfilled without considerable grassroots pressure. Until recently, human rights advocates have relied upon methods of "naming and shaming" government for failing to uphold human rights, raising societal awareness of violations, using test cases in courts, and conducting letter writing campaigns. But as efforts to realize economic and social rights have grown, and the breadth of human rights practitioners has expanded to include community organizers, these techniques and methods have broadened. Newer tactics include: engaging in rights-based impact assessments of policy, conducting budgetary analysis, and developing human rights indicators and benchmarks to measure the extent of effort a government expends to realize a given right. These new tools do not require advanced policy analysis expertise. Community organizers and local residents can embrace and use such methods with training (MacNaughton, 2011; UN Special Rapporteur on the Right to Health, 2007).

The ability to claim a right must also be accompanied by an understanding of who is responsible to protect or realize that right. According to Ife and Fisk (2006), "all human rights have individual and collective aspects," and human rights responsibilities similarly have individual and collective dimensions (p. 299). They join those who argue that responsibility for protecting and realizing human rights cannot be left to legal systems alone. Clearly, incorporating international human rights laws into domestic legal and policy-making practices is crucial to human rights work. Yet, changes in law alone do not necessarily lead to the realization of human rights. As they suggest in the example of anti-racist legislation, when such laws are passed advocates may feel that a major achievement has been gained and yet not fully realize that "anti-racist legislation alone will not eradicate racism" (p. 300). They find that "racism works in far more institutionalized and insidious ways to be eradicated by laws. Community-based education, consciousness-raising campaigns and ongoing movements at every level of society are needed to change public sentiment and values" (p. 299).

Efforts to realize human rights therefore require grassroots mobilization and engaged community-level practice (Onazi, 2013) to create what Wronka (2007) has called a human rights culture. Knowledge about human rights cannot be the domain solely of those involved in professions such as law, public health, and social work; it must also be fostered among the citizenry at large. This means that community practitioners are potentially important intermediaries between those who have typically been involved in human rights advocacy and monitoring and the broader public, a point which we develop throughout the book.

"American Exceptionalism" and the Struggle to Recognize Economic and Social Rights as Human Rights

The political quality of human rights work is no more evident than in the United States, where the seemingly simple task of *defining* human rights has been contested since the 1940s (Anderson, 2003; Armaline et al., 2011). The US government signed onto the Universal Declaration of Human Rights in 1948, signaling its recognition of the range of human rights principles contained in the treaty. Such support was grounded in considerable effort on the part of the federal government to overcome the economic hardships of the Great Depression and the excesses of two world wars. Yet since the inception of the United Nations, conservative and often overtly racist groups have attempted to block the United States from participating fully in the UN human rights system, especially in terms of social and economic rights (Anderson, 2003).

Opposition to recognizing economic and social rights has often been explained in the context of Cold War rivalries and anti-communism that prevailed in US political processes from the 1950s through the 1980s. Yet resistance to participation in the UN human rights system has as much to do with the legacy of federalism, the dominant ideology of "states' rights" and racism, and the belief that the United States is a land of opportunity where individuals can provide for themselves without assistance by federal or state government (Anderson, 2003; Rank, Hirschl, & Foster, 2014; Thomas, 2009). Resistance to social programs to promote the right to adequate housing, food, social protection, or education increased by the 1980s, just as social mobilization in the name of human rights began to flourish domestically and globally (Libal & Hertel, 2011).

This was a stark contrast—and reaction—to efforts in the 1960s to guarantee entitlement to aspects of economic and social rights (without utilizing such language). Spurred by grassroots mobilization and organizing by racial minorities and low-income groups for social inclusion, the federal government declared "War on Poverty." Marked by the expansion of existing and creation of new social welfare programs in education, housing, employment, and food security, and legal efforts to end segregation, the "American Dream" was opened up to millions of previously disenfranchised citizens. While key programs remain in place, the subsequent assault on these ideals ushered in an era of policy devolution and privatization, an offensive against organized labor, and a decline in the living standards of most income groups.

Human Rights and Social Work

International human rights norms and practices, often expressed in shorthand as "human rights law," have been a central aspect of international social work guidelines and principles for practice (United Nations Centre for Human Rights, 1994). The Statement of Ethical Principles adopted by the International Federation of Social Workers and the International Association of the Schools of Social Work (2004) stresses the importance of knowledge and practice based on human rights understandings. The Statement includes human rights and social justice as a core part of its definition of social work: "The social work profession promotes social change, problem solving in human relationships and the empowerment and liberation of people to enhance well-being. Utilising theories of human behaviour and social systems, social work intervenes at the points where people interact with their environments. Principles of human rights and social justice are fundamental to social work."

Domestically, human rights principles are also consonant with the National Association of Social Workers (NASW) Code of Ethics (2008), though the document does not explicitly invoke human rights (Steen, 2006). The Code of Ethics recognizes the primacy of the "dignity and worth of the person," social justice, and the importance of human relationships in its preamble, all of which are core aspects of human rights (NASW, 2008). The Code mandates social workers to "act to prevent and eliminate domination of, exploitation of, and discrimination against any person, group, or class on the basis of race, ethnicity, national origin, color, sex, sexual orientation, gender identity or expression, age, marital status, political belief, religion, immigration status, or mental or physical disability" (2008, 6.04). This provides clear linkage to human rights values of equality and non-discrimination and the responsibility of governments and other actors to assure these principles as a matter of human rights (MacNaughton, 2013).

The Congruence of Human Rights and Community Practice

Social work practice in the United States has a rich history of addressing problems and promoting change at the community level. The (eco-) systems perspective recognizes that environmental forces exert a key influence on the ability of families and individuals to function and thrive. Social problems that may manifest within individuals are thus seen as often embedded in key social institutions, structures, and policies. Understanding how social conditions create and contribute to personal and community problems therefore provides the basis for community practice. Inherent to this process has been a focus on building the capacity of communities to develop solutions to unjust conditions. This is linked to the "empowerment" perspective within macro practice—a focus on the need to promote feelings of self- and collective-efficacy in order to affect (change in) the socio-political environment (Gamble & Weil, 2010).

Macro practice has been defined as a purposeful effort to bring about change in organizations and communities (Netting, Kettner, McMurtry, & Thomas, 2011). A number of specific forms of community practice have also been articulated, including policy practice, political advocacy, community building, community development, community organizing, and radical community practice. While important distinctions exist within each in terms of tactics and constituencies, all share a commitment to some form of grassroots participation and a goal of promoting social inclusion.

Human rights practitioners at the United Nations, in collaboration with other stakeholders, have gradually identified cross-cutting principles in human rights practice. These are based upon the work of international and domestic human rights organizations and actors and have been outlined by the United Nations Special Rapporteur on Extreme Poverty and Human Rights (2013) in a report to the Human Rights Council. These overarching principles are: respect for dignity, autonomy, and agency; non-discrimination and equality; transparency and access to information; accountability; and empowerment. These ideas are also elaborated in the work of national-level human rights organizations, such as the National Economic and Social Rights Initiative in the United States, which also includes universality and indivisibility of human rights in its advocacy framework. As a whole, these ideas are central to rights-based practice. They offer a foundation from which to identify human rights concerns at a local, community, or state level, as well as a blueprint to develop indicators of progress to realize human rights. While a human rights framework addresses civil, political, economic, social, and cultural rights as indivisible, this book focuses on economic and social rights mobilization through community work.

Jewell et al. (2009) highlight the congruence of community organizing and human rights practice in their analysis of Women in Transition, created in the wake of welfare reform in 1998 by a group of welfare recipients attending university in Louisiville, Kentucky. They trace the organization's shift to using a rights-based perspective to address poverty, facilitated by their alliance with the Poor People's Economic Human Rights Campaign.

> Despite its neglected status within the social work curricula, community organizing for human rights pushes us closer to a just society in which those most affected by inequality and oppression open doors that had been closed to them in the public and political arenas. Community organizing for human rights must gain traction within the profession as the disparities between the haves and the have-nots continue to grow. Beyond simply valuing

> the concept of human rights, social workers must create the space needed for human rights organizing to be integrated and valued. (Jewell, et al., p. 319)

Fostering *participation* of affected or vulnerable groups is a core aspect of human rights-based practice. Community practice in the United States has long been predicated on the notion of meaningful participation within communities and in campaigns to create social change. As Ross (1955) noted in the 1950s, "people should participate in making, adjusting, or controlling the major changes taking place within their communities" (p. 89). Indeed, democracy as a political and social system requires "coöperative participation and action in the affairs of the community" (p. 91). Contemporary community practitioners have elaborated these basic principles to underscore core values of promoting social inclusion and civic engagement through efforts rooted in "everyday" forms of democracy. Such local practices entail fostering public engagement between elected officials, local professional elites, and individuals and groups most likely to benefit or be excluded from social policies and programs. Yet for those who are most marginalized within society, these ideals of participation are often not met.

Human rights theorists and practitioners increasingly have thus identified *participation itself* as a human right, and as a central factor in the realization of other human rights, such as the right to food, housing, or health care. The United Nations Special Rapporteur on Extreme Poverty and Human Rights suggests that for those who experience social exclusion, the right "to participate fully in society and in decision-making is blocked by multiple compounding obstacles—economic, social, structural, legal and systemic" (UN Special Rapporteur on Extreme Poverty and Human Rights, 2013, paragraph 13). Further:

> Material deprivation and disempowerment create a vicious cycle: the greater the inequality, the less participation; the less participation, the greater the inequality. When participation of people living in poverty is not actively sought and facilitated, they are not able to participate in decision-making and their needs and interests are not taken into account when policy is designed and implemented. (UN Special Rapporteur on Extreme Poverty and Human Rights, 2013, paragraph 14)

This cycle of exclusion deepens inequality, privileging elites or middle class groups who already command greater resources, influence over media and other venues for shaping policy. According to the Special Rapporteur Sepúlveda Carmona, "Conceived of as a right, participation is a means of challenging forms of domination that restrict people's agency and self-determination." Participation, she claims, should aim to be transformative rather than "'participatory' processes that are pro forma, tokenistic or undertaken to give predetermined policies a veneer of legitimacy" (United Nations Special Rapporteur on Extreme Poverty and Human Rights, 2013, paragraph 17). This latter point is crucial. Participation thus is not a means to an end (for example, securing the right to health or reduction of poverty), but is a fundamental human right itself (paragraph 19). As the Special Rapporteur asserts: "This right to take part and exert influence in decision-making processes that affect one's life is inextricably linked to the most fundamental understanding of being human and the purpose of rights: respect of dignity and the exercise of agency, autonomy and self-determination" (paragraph 20).

This right also corresponds to other core values consonant with community practice and social work in the United States, such as empowerment, the ability to exercise self-determination, and increase social capital. Moreover, it underscores the importance of action within groups or networks in solidarity to create more just social conditions (Barbera, 2014). As Sepúlveda Carmona concludes, "the enjoyment of the right to participation can benefit society as a whole, building trust and solidarity, creating better social cohesion and contributing to more inclusive and pluralistic societies, and bringing new issues and voices into the public arena" (United Nations Special Rapporteur on Extreme Poverty and Human Rights, 2013, paragraph 7).

Rights-Based Community Practice in a Neoliberal Era

A major barrier to rights-based practice in the United States is the dominance of market-based ideology which treats health care, housing, and food as commodities. As we show in this book, commodification of these essential aspects of life often results in the denial of key resources on a basis of equality. Neoliberal global economic policies have translated domestically into efforts to reduce the size and types of public entitlement programs over the past 35 years. In international law, such efforts are seen as retrogressive, undermining strides made in the 1960s and 1970s "War on Poverty" to make available affordable and decent housing, adequate food, and health care. As the National and Economic Social Rights Initiative has noted, "the United States largely relies on poorly regulated market mechanisms to satisfy fundamental needs, and treats the core goods, services, and infrastructure necessary for human well-being only as market commodities rather than public goods" (National Economic and Social Rights Initiative, 2010, p. 1).

Those at the forefront of human rights practice in the United States argue that powerful ideologies, such as racism and hyper-individualism, must be challenged in order to secure economic and social rights:

> [P]olitical culture and public policies in the United States cast human needs as private matters, and promote individual responsibility as a solution to problems arising from socio-economic determinants and persistent structural racism. This disproportionally hurts disadvantaged population groups, particularly low-income people and communities of color, yet the entire population suffers when the principle of collective action for the collective good is abandoned in favor of individual competition. (National Economic and Social Rights Initiative, 2010, p. 1)

This book is situated within a growing interest internationally and domestically to address poverty and inequality as human rights concerns in and of themselves. While global efforts to address poverty have focused on developing nations, increasingly the United Nations has asserted an obligation to address poverty in wealthy countries. The United States espouses greatness and even global supremacy, yet must also face the reality of widespread and persistent poverty; growing social inequality; high rates of unemployment and underemployment; low wages and weak social benefits for a large sector of the workforce; and rising costs of housing, health care, and nutritious foods (Rank et al., 2014). The country's enormous wealth and resources make it difficult to understand how more than 15 percent of the population, and 24 percent of children, are officially poor. The Copenhagen Declaration on Social Development and Programme of Action adopted by world leaders at the 1995 World Summit for Social Development states that

> poverty has various manifestations, including lack of income and productive resources sufficient to ensure sustainable livelihoods; hunger and malnutrition; ill health; limited or lack of access to education and other basic services; increased morbidity and mortality from illness; homelessness and inadequate housing; unsafe environments; and social discrimination and exclusion. It is also characterized by a lack of participation in decision-making and in civil, social and cultural life. (United Nations Department of Economic and Social Affairs, 1995, paragraph 19)

While this statement is global in its scope, its meaning is relevant for the United States. As the one of the wealthiest countries based on per capita gross domestic product (GDP) in the world, it is impossible to reconcile widespread failures to fulfill economic and human rights.[1] Describing contemporary US society, the Center for Economic and Social Rights (2010) found that more infants die before age one than in any other comparable country; women in the United States have the highest risk of dying in childbirth of any other high-income country in the Organisation for Economic Co-operation and Development (OECD); more than half of poorer Americans go without health care due to high costs; US social programs are "relatively ineffective at reducing inequality"; and systemic ethnic and racial disparities are evident in wages, access to adequate housing, and health care (pp. 2–6).

In 2003, Reichert contended that the social work profession was not yet well equipped to take a leadership role in human rights practice. More than 10 years after this claim, community-based social work is now well-situated to provide leadership and organizing in reframing core debates about social problems and human needs as matters of human rights.

> The elusive nature of equating social work with human rights appears to arise from the absence of a clear point of departure for social workers wishing to embrace human rights in their practice. If social work is a human rights profession, then where do social workers begin in applying human rights to practice? Where is the human rights compass to guide social workers? (Reichert, 2003, p. 232)

We argue that community practitioners have the capacity to integrate human rights into practice, particularly given the long-standing focus on fostering the participation of diverse stakeholders in any change effort. This book represents an effort to summarize key principles in human rights law and practice. In each of the

---

[1] The United States currently ranks 7th wealthiest in the world measured by per capita gross domestic product, taking into account an adjustment for purchasing power parity (PPP). See Global Finance (n.d.) for rankings based on International Monetary Fund figures.

following chapters, we address rights-based community practice through the lens of specific economic and social rights: health, housing, and food. This focus provides a "compass" to guide community practitioners in efforts to extend calls for social justice to include specific human rights principles and standards. Focusing on community practice through local and state-wide campaigns for different rights provides an in-depth illustration of how a particular right is defined and successful pathways of social and political action to secure that right. Throughout the book, we stress the interdependence of these rights and emphasize how the concept of participation is essential to human rights practice.

Each chapter introduces the reader to international human rights law; federal state and local policy and laws on the topic; a discussion of how laws and policies privilege some and disadvantage others within US society; and a consideration of how human rights-based approaches to health care, housing, and food can be used by community practitioners to catalyze social justice efforts.

Class Exercises and Additional Resources

The Universal Declaration of Human Rights (1948), Article 25

(1) Everyone has the right to a standard of living adequate for the health and well-being of himself and of his family, including food, clothing, housing and medical care and necessary social services, and the right to security in the event of unemployment, sickness, disability, widowhood, old age or other lack of livelihood in circumstances beyond his control.

(2) Motherhood and childhood are entitled to special care and assistance. All children, whether born in or out of wedlock, shall enjoy the same social protection.

US Participation in Human Rights Treaty Processes

United Nations Human Rights Treaties the United States Has Ratified

- Protocol Relating to the Status of Refugees (joined in 1968)
- Convention on the Prevention and Punishment of the Crime of Genocide (joined in 1988)
- International Covenant on Civil and Political Rights (joined in 1992)
- International Convention on the Elimination of All Forms of Racial Discrimination (joined in 1994)

- Convention against Torture and Other Cruel, Inhuman, or Other Degrading Forms of Treatment or Punishment (joined in 1994)
- Optional Protocol to the Convention on the Rights of the Child on the Sale of Children, Child Prostitution and Child Pornography (joined in 2002)
- Optional Protocol to the Convention on the Rights of the Child on the Involvement of Children in Armed Conflict (joined in 2002)

United Nations Human Rights Treaties the United States Has Not Ratified

- International Covenant on Economic, Social, and Cultural Rights
- Convention on the Elimination of All Forms of Discrimination Against Women
- Convention on the Rights of the Child
- International convention on the Protection of the Rights of All Migrant Workers and Members of Their Families
- Convention on the Rights of Persons with Disabilities
- International Convention for the Protection of All Persons from Enforced Disappearance

For Discussion: Is Extreme Poverty in the United States a Human Rights Violation?

The United Nations Independent Expert on the question of human rights and extreme poverty, Arjun Sengupta, visited the United States in 2005. During his ten-day visit, he met with government representatives and non-governmental organizations "working with and for people living in poverty." He held meetings in representative communities across the country, including New York City; Immokalee, Florida; New Orleans and Baton Rouge, Louisiana; Jackson and the Delta region of Mississippi; Appalachia (Kentucky); and Washington, D.C. Following investigations, Sengupta made the following comments and recommendations:

- Despite the economic wealth of the United States and the efforts of the Government, the poverty rate remains high compared to other rich nations and there is no evidence that the incidence of poverty, and especially extreme poverty, is on the decrease;
- Government programmes and policies have not effectively remedied the vulnerable situation of those groups most at risk of extreme poverty, notably African Americans, Hispanics, immigrants, and women single-headed households;
- There is no national anti-poverty legislation in the United States. There is only a patchwork of different laws addressing aspects of poverty in a limited manner;

- If the United States adopted a comprehensive national strategy and programmes based on human rights principles, it would be possible to reduce poverty and eradicate extreme poverty;
- Social safety nets for poor families should be through entitlement programmes, and measures should be taken to facilitate the participation in these programmes and ensure that cumbersome enrollment procedures do not discourage people who qualify for social benefits from applying;
- The full participation of people living in poverty should be ensured in the design, implementation, monitoring, and assessment of programmes for combating poverty. Such programmes should build on poor people's own efforts, ensuring the full participation of the people concerned and responding to their actual needs.

The United States is encouraged to adopt the following steps: First, the United States authorities, in cooperation with civil society and expert organizations, should identify a fraction of its population as suffering from conditions of extreme poverty (defined in terms of a combination of income poverty, human development poverty, and social exclusion). Second, once this group has been identified, the United States authorities should adopt legislative provisions to accord them the legal entitlement to the programmes that are needed to take them out of these conditions of poverty. This legal entitlement would allow extremely poor persons, or their representatives, to seek redress in the courts if they are denied their entitlements. Third, in order to fund such programmes, the federal Government may create a fund with the sole purpose of abolishing the conditions of extreme poverty (excerpted from the UN Independent Expert on the Question of Human Rights and Extreme Poverty, 2005, p. 2).

Questions for Discussion

- In small groups identify which of the recommendations you consider to be consistent with social work values and ethics.
- As community practitioners, how might you integrate these findings and recommendations into your advocacy for persons living in poverty?
- What steps would you take to create a national campaign to eradicate poverty?

For Discussion: My Voice Counts—The Human Right to Participate

The following was published on the Office of the High Commissioner for Human Rights Web site in recognition of Human Rights Day on December 10, 2012. The focus of the 2012 Human Rights Day was "Inclusion and the Right to Participate in Public Life." Social inclusion and public participation extends far beyond exercising one's right to vote in elections. It entails having access to and being heard in a range of public settings, often at the community level. Everyday Democracy (www.everydaydemocracy.org) is an example of a group that seeks to foster such inclusive participation in community life. While in the United States this is often cast as civic engagement, it is directly linked to the right participate in public life as a human right. Read the following statement excerpted from the Office of the High Commissioner for Human Rights briefing on the 2012 Human Rights Day and discuss the questions that follow.

Everybody has the right to have their voice heard and to have a role in making the decisions that shape their communities. Each one of us should be able to choose those people who will represent us in all governance institutions, to stand for public office, and to vote on the fundamental questions that shape our individual and collective destinies.

The return on that investment is a society tuned to the needs and aspirations of its constituents. Where this fundamental right is respected, each and every one of us is offered the opportunity to join in the debate, to offer ideas, to campaign for change —to participate.

Fulfillment of the right to participate in public life is fundamental to the functioning of a democratic society and an effective human rights protection system. Inclusion of ALL in decision-making processes is an essential precondition to the achievement of both.

Millions of people have gone onto the streets in the past few years to have their say, to protest the unyielding, unresponsive governments which have shut them out. They have demanded and continue demanding respect for their fundamental human rights, including their right to have a voice and for that voice to count.

Elsewhere, many remain silent, unable to take any part in the public lives of their communities. Often they cannot stand for office, vote for public officials or in referenda: at times they are prohibited from expressing their views at all.

Women, people with disabilities, individuals belonging to minorities and indigenous peoples, the poor, those with little or no education, remote rural communities, continue to be disenfranchised in many places, sometimes even prohibited from participation in public life or excluded on the basis of discriminatory laws or practices or because there is no appropriate infrastructure which would facilitate their inclusion.

The focus of this year's Human Rights Day refers directly to the articles in the Universal Declaration of Human Rights which provide for the right to freedom of assembly and association, the right to take part in elections, in public life and decision-making institutions and the right to freedom of expression and opinion.

These values, endorsed by the international community, are legally binding obligations upon the 167 States Parties to the International Covenant on Civil and Political Rights which stipulates that the right to participate in the conduct of public affairs applies to "every citizen without exception."

In the face of the extraordinary contemporary challenges for democracy, climate change, globalization, the on-going economic and financial crises in many countries, and the explosion of global Web-based communication, among others, participation and inclusion are critical in the development and implementation of durable, workable policy solutions.

Your voice, your right. Your voice counts ....

(Excerpted from: Office of the High Commissioner for Human Rights, http://www.ohchr.org/EN/NewsEvents/Day2012/Pages/HRDay2012Intro.aspx).

Questions for Discussion

- What does *meaningful participation* in community and public life mean?
- What barriers exist for low income or other marginalized groups to participate in local, state, or national decision-making processes?
- Is participation in governance and decision-making a human right? Why or why not?
- What are some examples of effective participation by low income or marginalized individuals and groups?

Organizations Engaged in Human Rights-Based Practice in the United States

The following is a list of organizations that focus efforts on social and economic rights mobilization at national, state, and local levels. Some, like the US Human Rights Network, represent coalitions of hundreds of other groups. As the movement expands, the list of organizations also grows.

- Amnesty International USA: http://www.amnestyusa.org/
- Everyday Democracy: http://everyday-democracy.org/
- Heartland Alliance: Ending Poverty: http://www.heartlandalliance.org/
- Human Rights Watch: http://www.hrw.org/
- National Economic and Social Rights Initiative: http://www.nesri.org/
- Southern Poverty Law Center: http://www.splcenter.org/
- The Opportunity Agenda: http://opportunityagenda.org/
- The Poor People's Economic Human Rights Campaign: http://economichumanrights.org/
- The Poverty Initiative: http://www.povertyinitiative.org/
- Urban Justice: http://www.urbanjustice.org/
- US Human Rights Network: http://www.ushrnetwork.org/
- Vermont Workers Center: http://www.workerscenter.org/
- Witness: http://www.witness.org/.

Chapter 2
Mobilizing for the Right to Health and Health Care

We really need to stop thinking of health care as a for-profit venture and start treating it as a right and a public good.
—Franzen, as cited in NESRI (2010, p. 9)

Human rights advocates, like Peg Franzen of the Vermont Workers' Center, view corporate profit-making in the health sector and realizing the human right to health care as fundamentally incompatible. This is especially relevant in the United States when the success of health policy is measured predominantly in terms of profitability and cost-benefit analyses rather than positive health outcomes for all people. Since the early 1990s local and national efforts in the United States have sought to redefine health care not as a commodity, but as a human right (McGill, 2012; Soohoo & Goldberg, 2010). Labor organizers, public interest lawyers, community leaders, and social workers have increasingly challenged the commodification of health through grassroots advocacy, with an aim to change state and federal health policy. Their fundamental goal is to address the lack of universal access to affordable, quality health care.

The US health care system is often touted as offering a level of care unsurpassed by any other country. Indeed, the United States spends over twice as much per capita on health care as the average developed country.[1] Others suggest that the *quality* of health goods and services in the United States is also superior. Yet the National Research Council and Institute of Medicine of the National Academies (Woolf & Aron, 2013) recently acknowledged that the United States falls far short of having the world's best health care system. Indeed, a growing body of evidence points to another way in which the United States is "exceptional" among its peers, but in this instance it is in terms of "health disadvantage" (2013, p. 4). Health outcomes and access to health care highlight pervasive inequality and health disparities in the United States. In 2010, for example, a record 50 million people (approximately 16 % of the US population) lacked health insurance (US Census Bureau, 2012).

---

[1] Per capita health care expenditures in 2011 were $8,508 in the United States, compared to $3,322 on average for Organisation for Economic Co-Operation and Development (OECD) countries (Organisation for Economic Co-Operation and Development, n.d.).

K.R. Libal and S. Harding, *Human Rights-Based Community Practice in the United States*, SpringerBriefs in Rights-Based Approaches to Social Work,
DOI 10.1007/978-3-319-08210-3_2

The number without health coverage was significantly higher among non-whites/racial minorities, lower-income workers, and those who worked less than full-time (and non-workers). Access to health insurance in the United States is also determined by geography: the percent of the (non-elderly) population lacking health insurance is highest in the South and Southwest (Solomon, 2013). Despite improvements in access to health insurance in 2011 and 2012, the period from 1999–2010 witnessed a marked decline in health insurance coverage for most groups (US Census Bureau, 2012; Center on Budget and Policy Priorities, 2013c). Tyler (2013) notes that while the Patient Protection and Affordable Care Act of 2010 (hereafter ACA) is intended to significantly expand coverage to the uninsured and underinsured, its passage "will not end the debate in America about the need for the realization of the right to health care" (pp. 80–81). Expanding health care insurance alone will not be sufficient to overcome decades-long legacies of disparities in access health care services and health outcomes.

Data on health insurance finds a direct connection between social class—and often, poverty—and health coverage. In the United States, the intersections with race and ethnicity and gender are crucial to consider; health disparities are systemic, affecting people of color disproportionately on major measures of health and well-being. In general, individuals and those living in households with higher incomes have better health outcomes and live longer. The United States Centers for Disease Control and Prevention (2013) reports that health disparities persist throughout the country in numerous domains. As one example, they illustrate the importance of poverty status or membership in an ethnic group as a determinant of access to health care (United States Centers for Disease Control and Prevention, 2013). According to Wolfe (2012), "those with low incomes also tend to have relatively poor outcomes for health and mortality, compared to those with higher incomes. The gap appears to begin prior to birth, and then increase throughout childhood" (p. 25).

As troubling, a 2013 study found inferior health outcomes in the United States compared to 16 comparable or "peer" high-income countries (Woolf & Aron, 2013). Examining data from the 1990s–2008, compared with the average of peer countries, the United States fared worse in nine health domains:

- adverse birth outcomes; injuries and homicides
- adolescent pregnancy and sexually transmitted infections
- HIV and AIDS
- drug-related mortality
- obesity and diabetes
- heart disease
- chronic lung disease
- disability status related to aging.

The US health disadvantage affects all groups, and while it is "more pronounced among socioeconomically disadvantaged groups … even advantaged Americans appear to fare worse than their counterparts in England and some other countries" (Woolf & Aron 2013, p. 3). The authors underscore that the "health disadvantage is particularly striking given the wealth and assets of the United States and the country's enormous level of per capita spending on health care, which far exceeds that of any other country" (p. 4).

A particular challenge in the United States is the patchwork of policies and programs to provide health care insurance coverage and health services access. This includes employer-based insurance programs which have significant variability in levels of coverage and costs. Public programs, including Medicaid, Medicare, the Children's Health Insurance Program (CHIP), and health programs for some veterans available through the American Veteran's Alliance, also address health needs of targeted individuals. Medicaid is a federal-state public insurance program providing health coverage to nearly 65 million low-income Americans (including children, adults, the elderly, and persons with disabilities) (Center on Budget and Policy Priorities, n.d.). The Children's Health Insurance Program (CHIP) gives states matching federal funds to provide health coverage to nearly 8 million children in families whose income is typically up to 200 % of the poverty line. Medicare is a federal program providing health coverage to about 47 million Americans (in general, over 65 years old and including several million younger adults with disabilities). It is estimated that the Affordable Care Act of 2010 will help nearly 32 million uninsured Americans obtain quality, affordable health coverage in both the private and public markets.

Despite these numerous programs, the health sector is fragmented and still excludes many Americans (both low and medium income) from quality health services. The US health care system includes profit-based insurance and health service delivery and non-profit and/or "charity care" (Goodnough, 2014). It is in this context that we argue that addressing US health disadvantage is a matter of human rights. Tyler (2013) claims to "successfully frame a health and human rights strategy in the US, it is essential that the health care, public health, and legal communities unite to effect change at the community as well as the state and national levels" (81). Social workers can play a central role in such a mobilization as well. Local, state, and national organizing for the right to health and health care has revitalized earlier efforts in US history to achieve universal health care. During the same period in which the Universal Declaration of Human Rights was adopted by the United Nations and the UN Commission for Human Rights worked to further define a right to health and health care, in the United States the Roosevelt, Truman and Johnson administrations sought to implement a universal health insurance program (Rudiger & Meier, 2003). Though President Johnson failed to articulate health care as a right, his policies "advanced the principle of government responsibility to actualize social and economic rights through his comprehensive efforts to address poverty, improve educational opportunity, expand affordable housing, and provide improved social services to disadvantaged American citizens through his War on Poverty and Great Society programs" (Schimmel, 2013, p. 5).

Despite presidential support for enacting a universal health care plan, the American Medical Association (AMA), representing interests of physicians, argued that universal health care schemes being implemented in Europe threatened core values of "personal freedom." Using the specter of Cold War-era politics, the AMA claimed the Truman administration's recognition of "access to the means for the attainment and preservation of health" as a "basic human right" would lead to "socialized medicine" and was contradictory to core American norms about choice (President's Commission on the Health Needs of the Nation as cited in Rudiger and Meier (2003), p. 72).[2] Contemporary debates about health care access still mirror these cleavages.

In the following pages, we highlight prominent examples of efforts to challenge the dominant framework of health care-as-commodity to illustrate how local, community-based mobilization can contribute to a broader national dialogue on health justice. This chapter depicts the importance of community practice to the realization of the human right to health and health care. Community practitioners can help assure the participation of vulnerable and affected groups in mobilizing for rights-based approaches to health care, develop programs and policies responsive to local communities, and promote accountability and transparency in health care provision through broad public engagement. We link the conceptual framework of community practice, focusing on political and social action outlined by Gamble and Weil (2010), with human rights-based mobilization for health and health services. Emphasis is placed on the importance of fostering broad participation in social and political campaigns to affect policy change.

Defining the Right to Health and Health Care: International Standards and Practices

The "right to enjoyment of the highest attainable standard of physical and mental health" was established in international law in the 1946 Constitution of the World Health Organization (WHO) (World Health Organization, 2005 [1946]), even before the adoption of the Universal Declaration of Human Rights (1948). According to the WHO Constitution, health is "a state of complete physical, mental and social well-being and not merely the absence of disease or infirmity." The Preamble of this Constitution further asserts that "the enjoyment of the highest attainable standard of health is one of the fundamental rights of every human being without distinction of race, religion, political belief, economic or social condition" (World Health Organization, 2005 [1946]). The right to health was also invoked as part of the right to an adequate standard of living in the UDHR (Art. 25) and was recognized as a human right in the International Covenant on Economic, Social and Cultural Rights (ICESCR) in 1966. It is also referenced in all the other major human rights treaties.

Since the founding of the United Nations in 1945, the meaning of the right to the highest attainable standard of health has gradually been elaborated. In particular, the

[2] Today the American Medical Association (n.d.) invokes the responsibility of medical professionals to "advocate for social, economic, educational, and political changes that ameliorate suffering and contribute to human well-being" and highlights that these "responsibilities confer on physicians an active obligation to respect and advocate for the human rights of their patients and society, as a means to promoting good health."

Committee on Economic, Social, and Cultural Rights (which monitors the treaty) and a UN Special Rapporteur on the right to health have helped define the obligations of governments and other non-governmental organizations in respecting, protecting, and fulfilling the right to health. In 2000, the UN Committee on Economic, Social, and Cultural Rights issued General Comment No. 14 on the right to the highest attainable standard of health, providing important depth to understanding the right to health. While the United States has yet to join the ICESCR (1966), and thus is not bound to its provisions in international human rights law, the guidelines provided in General Comment No. 14 and in other human rights documentation provide a strong basis for advocacy and policy-making.

The ICESCR establishes that parties to the treaty "recognize the right of everyone to the enjoyment of the highest attainable standard of physical and mental health" (1966, paragraph 12.1). Moreover, governments are to formulate and implement policies that include efforts to reduce infant mortality and promote child development; improve "environmental and industrial hygiene"; prevent, treat, and control disease; and create conditions to "assure to all medical service and medical attention in the event of an illness" (paragraph 12.2a–d). This articulation of the right to health also includes a right to the "enjoyment of a variety of facilities, goods, services and conditions necessary for the realization of the highest attainable standard of health" (UN CESCR, 2000, paragraph 9).

Core Principles of the Right to Health and Health Care

International human rights law establishes that the right to health is an "inclusive right" that contains both freedoms and entitlements (Office of the United Nations High Commissioner for Human Rights and the World Health Organisation, n.d.). The right to health is expansive—broader than a right to health care—as it is predicated on the realization of other human rights, including adequate housing, food, water, education, and a range of civil and political rights (Hunt & Backman, 2008).

Securing the right to health, which has been criticized by some as overly broad[3] is firmly entwined with a subset of this right to access a "variety of facilities, goods, services" (CESCR, 2000, paragraph 9). This entails addressing the right to access health care and a system of health care delivery that is based upon four essential components: the availability, accessibility, acceptability, and quality of health services (CESCR, 2000, paragraph 12). Access to these elements can be assessed through several questions. First, in terms of *availability*, does a functioning public health and health care system exist, including goods and services, plentiful enough to assure that all individuals can make use of them on a basis of non-discrimination? Second, are the existing health facilities, goods, and services accessible to everyone? This notion of *accessibility* includes four aspects: (1) non-discrimination; (2) physical

[3] See Wolff (2012) for a helpful overview of this critique.

accessibility; (3) economic accessibility or affordability; and (4) information accessibility (World Health Organisation, 2008). Third, the right to health care also requires attention to whether or not health facilities, goods, and services meet the standard of *acceptability*. Thus, are they "respectful of medical ethics and culturally appropriate, i.e., respectful of the culture of individuals, minorities, peoples and communities, sensitive to gender and life-cycle requirements" (UN CESCR, 2000, paragraph 12c)? Fourth, the right to health care requires that health facilities, goods, and services must be "scientifically and medically appropriate and of good quality." In other words, in assessing *quality* are there "skilled medical personnel, scientifically approved and unexpired drugs and hospital equipment, safe and potable water, and adequate sanitation" (paragraph 12d)?

The right to health embodies all the above principles in terms of health care facilities, goods, and services, but it also has a more expansive dimension that recognizes that health is affected by underlying social determinants. The social determinants of health have been defined as "the circumstances in which people are born, grow up, live, work and age, and the systems put in place to deal with illness. These circumstances are in turn shaped by a wider set of forces: economics, social policies, and politics" (World Health Organization, n.d., p. 1). These social determinants of health are defined in human rights terms as being secured by the realization of social, economic, cultural, civil and political rights which are understood as *interdependent*. Thus, as the UN Committee on Economic, Social, and Cultural Rights (2000) suggests:

> The right to health is closely related to and dependent upon the realization of other human rights, as contained in the International Bill of Rights, including the rights to food, housing, work, education, human dignity, life, non-discrimination, equality, the prohibition against torture, privacy, access to information, and the freedoms of association, assembly and movement. These and other rights and freedoms address integral components of the right to health (paragraph 3).

International human rights law recognizes that realizing economic and social rights requires the input of resources to fulfill the government's obligations in these domains. Human rights, in short, involve not only the *claims* of rights-holders, but also the *obligations* of duty-bearers (in this instance, the government).

A number of other dimensions of the right to health and health care must be understood in order to develop effective advocacy. The first is that the right to health is to be progressively realized, which means that governments must demonstrate that they are taking steps toward the full achievement of the right. Some governments may not be able to immediately foster the realization of all dimensions of the right to adequate health due to weaknesses in existing health care systems, insufficient economic resources, and/or inadequate capacity. Nonetheless, the Committee on Economic and Social Rights in recent years has underscored that the notion of "progressive realization" of the right to health should not be taken as a license for states to act slowly in prioritizing policies and programs. In addition, countries not facing serious resource constraints are held to a higher standard for implementing the right expediently. Thus, under international law, the United States is understood to have adequate resources and expertise to design and implement health care systems to fulfill a universal right to health and health care (MacNaughton, 2012).

Governments, regardless of resources, must also demonstrate that they are "taking steps" to realize the right to health. This means, at a minimum, governments must:

(1) Adopt a "national strategy to ensure to all the enjoyment of the right to health, based on human rights principles which define the objectives of the strategy";
(2) Set indicators and benchmarks for the "formulation and implementation" of the strategy; and
(3) Address the "core minimum obligation" which includes: (a) "[A]ccess to health facilities, goods and services *on a non-discriminatory basis*, especially for vulnerable or marginalized groups"; (b) "Access to the *minimal essential food* which is nutritiously adequate and safe"; (c) "Access to *shelter, housing and sanitation* and an adequate supply of safe drinking water"; (d) "The provision of *essential drugs*"; and (e) "*Equitable distribution* of all health facilities, goods and services" (World Health Organisation, 2008, pp. 24–25).

The latter set of core minimum obligations illustrates the notion of interdependence of rights, suggesting that access to health care by itself is no guarantee of good health if individuals and groups face barriers to housing, food, or income. In international law, governments are obliged to "take steps towards the realization of rights, including the right to health, which should be *concrete, deliberate, and targeted*" (Emphasis ours, WHO, 2008, p. 24).

The progressive realization principle affords government time to implement programs and policies to realize the right to health or other economic and social rights. But, when discrimination on the basis of factors, such as race, ethnicity, sex, sexual orientation, language, religion, political or other opinion, national or social origin, or ability status, has the "intention or effect of nullifying or impairing the equal enjoyment or exercise of the right to health" then government must take affirmative steps to end such discrimination immediately (UN Committee on Social and Economic Rights, 2000, paragraph 18). The UN Committee on Social and Economic Rights further underscores that "health facilities, goods and services must be accessible to all, especially the most vulnerable or marginalized sections of the population, in law and in fact, without discrimination on any of the prohibited grounds" (2000, paragraph 12c).

The question of discrimination is particularly profound in the United States, where health disparities on the basis of race and gender are well documented (CERD Working Group on Health and Environmental Health, 2008). The US government's latest report to the Committee on the Elimination of Racial Discrimination openly admitted that despite efforts to enforce the laws such as the Civil Rights Act of 1964, which prohibits discrimination in federally funded hospitals and health care centers, health disparities "based on race and ethnicity, socioeconomic status and other factors persist at unacceptably high levels" (United States Department of State, 2013, paragraph 133).

Rights-based mobilization for health in the United States also entails the broad-based *participation* of multiple stakeholders, but especially of individuals and groups affected by exclusion from the "core minimum obligations" above. Moreover, human rights law mandates that when racial and ethnic disparities are present, governments, such as the United States, are to implement laws and practices that redress these inequalities immediately. In the face of undeniable racial and ethnic health disparities—which the US government itself admits—the role for grassroots involvement in formulation and implementation of the right to health care is crucial. Only through such participation can accountability for realizing the right health and health care be fostered.

U.S. Obligations for Securing the Right to Health and Health Care

The United States has failed to ratify several key human rights treaties that articulate a right to health and health care services.[4] These include the International Covenant on Economic, Social, and Cultural Rights (ICESCR) (1966), the Convention on the Elimination of All Forms of Discrimination Against Women (CEDAW) (1979), the Convention on the Rights of the Child (CRC) (1989), the Convention on the Protection of Rights of All Migrant Workers and Members of Their Families (1990), and the Convention on the Rights of Persons with Disabilities (2006).[5] However, the United States has signed the ICESCR, CEDAW, and the CRC, which obligates the government to "refrain from acts that would defeat the object and purpose" of the treaties (MacNaughton, 2011, p. 212). Furthermore, the United States has joined several human rights treaties which outline the intersection of civil and political rights and rights to health and health care services, especially with respect to special or minority populations, or individuals under the guardianship of the state (prisoners, migrants held in detention, refugees, youth in state care).[6] The US government has also acknowledged economic and

[4] Joining an international human rights treaty in the case of the United States entails a process whereby the President signs a treaty, signaling endorsement of its principles. Lawyers for the State Department then analyze the treaty. Following that review, the administration forwards recommendations to the Senate Foreign Relations Committee concerning any aspects of the treaty to which the government claims reservations or understandings. If ratified, the United States may officially file such reservations with the treaty body (Venitis, 2011). The Senate Foreign Relations Committee determines whether or not to advance a treaty to the full body of the Senate for debate and a vote. A two-thirds vote of the Senate is necessary to approve a treaty, followed by the President's final signature.

[5] In late 2013, the Senate Foreign Relations Committee pushed for a second vote in the Senate to ratify the Convention on the Rights of Persons with Disabilities, which was defeated by just six votes earlier in the year (Cox & Pequet, 2012). This is the first human rights treaty that has been seriously considered for ratification in the United States since 1994.

[6] These include the International Covenant on Civil and Political Rights (1966), the Convention Against Torture (1984), and, importantly, the Convention on the Elimination of All Forms of Racial Discrimination (1965).

social rights by inviting UN Special Rapporteurs on education, housing, water, and extreme poverty to the United States to investigate claims of human rights violations in these areas. And, in 2010, the United States highlighted the Patient Protection and Affordable Care act in its Universal Periodic Review report to the Human Rights Council, signaling its belief that this policy addressed health care as a human right (United States Department of State, 2010).

Greater receptivity in the United States to engaging on social and economic rights issues, despite the legacy of weak constitutional supports for such rights, is due largely to growing social and political pressure. In the past 20 years, civil society organizations have begun to invoke the right to health and health care services in advocacy campaigns. Local groups have creatively used international human rights monitoring processes linked to reporting on key global treaties to address some aspects of the right to health and health care (as noted in the discussion of CERD above). Advocates have focused on issues that intersect with civil and political rights, particularly related to obligations of the government to refrain from violating the right to health in terms of torture, and inhumane or degrading treatment and punishment within the military and criminal justice system (CUNY School of Law and American Civil Liberties Union, n.d.; International Human Rights Law Clinic University of Chicago Law, Chicago Legal Advocacy for Incarcerated Mothers, and American Civil Liberties Union 2013). Activists have also used provisions of the right to health and health care on the basis of equality under the International Convention on the Elimination of All Forms of Racial Discrimination, drawing attention to disparate health outcomes on the basis of race and ethnicity as a human rights concern (CERD Working Group on Health and Environmental Health, 2008; Human Rights Project of the Urban Justice Center, 2007).

Despite the US failure to ratify key treaties that involve the right to health care, advocates have used the moral weight of human rights framing, as well as the standards set by the Committee for Social, Economic, and Cultural Rights and the Special Rapporteur on the right to health, to make rights-based claims. Such efforts have taken place in varied contexts: at local levels in terms of seeking to influence municipal policy (King County/Seattle or Baltimore, MD), at the state level (Vermont, Maine, Maryland, and Pennsylvania) and to a lesser degree nationally (McGill, 2012; Rudiger, 2011; Solomon, 2009).

A major impediment to realizing robust, universal rights-based standards for health care is the fact that there is no constitutional right to health in the United States outside of efforts to address discrimination on the basis of being in a protected class (Carmalt, Zaidi, & Yamin, 2011; Swendiman, 2012). While there has been some interest in Congress in a Constitutional amendment to make health and health care a matter of rights enforceable on the basis of the US Constitution, these efforts have had little practical impact. The Congressional Research Service recently commissioned an analysis of Supreme Court decisions related to health care in an effort to outline the relationship between health care and the Constitution (Swendiman, 2012). The first sentence of the study invokes many of the principles of a rights-based approach to health care. It states: "The health care reform debate raises many complex issues including those of coverage, accessibility, cost, accountability, and quality of health care. Underlying these policy considerations are issues regarding the status of health or health care as a moral, legal, or constitutional right" (2012, p. 1). At stake is the issue of whether or not the court would find an "implicit fundamental right to health care for poor persons under the Constitution" (p. 2). The authors of the report pose the following questions: "If each individual has a right to health care, how much care does a person have a right to and from whom? Would equality of access be a component of such a right? Do federal or state governments have a duty to provide health care services to the large numbers of medically uninsured persons? What kind of health care system would fulfill a duty to provide health care? How should this duty be enforced?" (2012, p. 2).

That these questions have been posed for a Congressional audience suggests that social mobilization for a rights-based approach to health care has gained influence in the United States.[7] However, the framing of any duty or obligation to health care is narrow, at least to date. The Congressional report argues that though the United States Constitution "does not explicitly set forth a right to health care, the Supreme Court's decisions in the areas of right to privacy and bodily integrity suggest the Constitution implicitly provides an individual the right to access health care services at *one's own expense* from willing medical providers" (emphasis ours, Swendiman, 2012, p. 2). It also asserts, however, that if the Supreme Court in the future were to find an "implicit right to health care for persons unable to pay for such care, it might do so either by finding that the Constitution implicitly guarantees such a right, or that a law which treats persons differently based on financial need creates a 'suspect classification'" (p. 2). The report underscores that either of these pathways to legal recognition of a fundamental right to health care for those who cannot afford such services is possible, but does not speculate on whether or not the current Supreme Court would make such a finding.

Despite the lack of constitutional protections and Supreme Court interpretations that recognize a right to health care, the United States has enacted policies in the past 50 years that are consonant with some of the values of the right to the highest attainable standard of health. These include statues such as Title VI of the Civil Rights Act of 1964 (42 U.S.C. section 2000d) and the creation of social policies providing more accessibility to health care goods and services. In 1965, Congress created Medicare (a program addressing older adult health care) and Medicaid (to provide basic health services to people with very low incomes). The Civil Rights Act of 1964 meant that hospitals receiving federal Medicare funds must integrate and demonstrate that they were not discriminating against patients (Bonastia, 2006). Other laws also sought to expand access to health care, including the Mental Health Parity Act of 1996 and the State Children's Health Insurance Program (SCHIP) of 1997. While

---

[7] MacNaughton and McGill (2012) point to a trend in the United States to implement economic and social rights without ratification of international treaties. We argue that rights-based concepts and benchmarks, such as accessibility and affordability, as well as quality health care, have made their way into *the practice* of health care policy-making. While the duties to fulfill or realize these dimensions for all remain unmet, key norms have begun to shift where such claims are made in varied settings (in Congress, at the state level, and in local organizing).

these were important legislative steps, they often devolved responsibility for implementation of programs to the state level and failed to meet human rights standards which entailed universal coverage and access to quality health care. Further, despite the much-touted reforms of the 2010 Patient Protection and Affordable Care Act (ACA), designed to provide greater access to health insurance and health care benefits, the law fails to meet human rights-based standards (Carmalt et al., 2011; Tyler, 2013; Schimmel, 2013).

The United States is the only wealthy, industrialized country in the world that does not provide a plan for universal health care coverage and does not recognize a legal right to care, except in emergency situations (Yamin, 2005). Even passage of the ACA will not provide universal health coverage to all people in the United States. The law's provisions favor "expansion of the market-based health insurance system over universal coverage, failing to fully address the existing problems with access to health care for the underserved" (Tyler, 2013, p. 84). The Supreme Court's decision in *National Federation of Independent Business v. Sebelius* (2012) permits states to determine Medicaid eligibility standards and whether or not to participate in Medicaid expansion. The "flexibility" given to states as a result of this ruling has resulted in the exclusion of an estimated 6 million of potential beneficiaries in states that did not elect for Medicaid expansion (Kaiser Commission on the Medicaid and the Uninsured, 2013).

The Central Role of Community Practice in Securing the Right to Health Care

Realizing the human right to health care presents challenges in any national context, but in the United States this dilemma is amplified by longstanding practices of administering health policy at the state level. The federal system presents barriers to achieving universal access to affordable, quality health care services on a basis of equality and non-discrimination. While a large percentage of US citizens realize a high standard of access to health services, the US health care system is inherently unequal and millions of people have limited access to even the most basic health care services (Carmalt et al., 2011; Hoffman, 2012). Even experts who have lauded the 2010 health care reform recognize that its effects could be limited and not achieve universal goals that are required from a right to health approach (Gable, 2011).

The Affordable Care Act does establish a "legal infrastructure that seeks to achieve universal health insurance coverage" and "targets some of the major impediments to accessing needed health care for millions of Americans" (Gable, 2011, p. 340). These include not only health insurance exchanges and efforts to control costs of health care services, but also an expansion of public health infrastructure, clinical and community preventative services, and efforts to educate the public in preventative health measures, particularly linked to diet, obesity, and prevention of chronic disease. Addressing each of these domains of the ACA from a rights-based approach to health requires *participation* of individuals. Arguably the "affected population" in this context is a large proportion of society which has limited access to health care services for either prevention or treatment. Community practitioners thus have a substantial role to play in helping communities to assess changes being wrought under the law, the effects of this policy on individuals, families and communities, and in developing local and national responses to limitations in the implementation of the ACA in the future.

Beyond the ACA: State-Level Advocacy for the Human Right to Health Care

Community or "macro" practice is one of the oldest methods of social work in the United States. This includes different forms of practice in communities (community organizing, community development, and community building), as well as policy advocacy and policy practice, planning, and activities performed within organizations. Despite a variety of possible practice roles and modes of engagement, community practice is generally viewed as focused on efforts to address social problems and promote social change. Until recently, linking community practice to human rights in the United States was rare (e.g., Androff, 2012; Jewell, Collins, Gargotto, & Dishon, 2009; Pyles, 2006). Drawing upon the model for social and political action developed by Gamble and Weil (2010), we highlight cases of rights-based mobilization for health and health services in the United States and illustrate the potential of infusing core principles of the right to health care within community practice. These examples suggest both the opportunities and challenges of "grass-roots" campaigning for the right to health services in the United States.

An important mode of community practice is grounded in political and social action; the aim of this form of community organizing is to mobilize various constituencies for broad social and political aims (Gamble & Weil, 2010). Such engagement is evident in the work of the Vermont Workers' Center (VWC) in its efforts to create the first state law "for a universal, publicly financed health care system" (Rudiger, 2011).[8] The VWC initiated its "Healthcare Is a Human Right" campaign in 2008. By 2011, in collaboration with other community groups, they secured the adoption of Act 128 and Act 48, which incorporated human rights principles into Vermont law and provided a framework for creating a state-funded health care program that assures all Vermont residents access to quality health care (McGill, 2012).

The VWC's campaign used an explicit human rights frame, drawing upon the principles of universality, equity, transparency, accountability, and participation. According to McGill, the campaign emphasized that:

---

[8] The group started out in 1996 as the Central Vermonters for a Livable Wage and officially became the Vermont Workers' Center in 1998. They first established a Workers' Rights Hotline and devoted much of the first decade of work to workers' rights. By 2008, the VWC shifted to health care as a primary campaign out of recognition that health care access was a key concern for many members of the Center (http://www.workerscenter.org/about-vermont-workers-center/history).

> health care should be available to all Vermonters regardless of their ability to pay; that the cost of the health care system should be shared fairly; that Vermonters should participate in the design and implementation of the health care system; that the system should be transparent, efficient, and accountable to the people it serves; and that the government should be responsible for ensuring that the health care system complies with these principles (2012, p. 108).

Organizers for the Health is Human Right Campaign held public meetings throughout the state between 2008 and 2010, raising awareness about the failures of the Vermont health care system and principles of a human rights-based approach to health care. Supporters believed that mobilizing local residents was crucial to any substantive health policy reform. They focused on engaging a broad group of supporters, due a failed attempt to pass single-payer health care in 2005, when Republican Governor James Douglas vetoed the legislation. As one organizer noted, "We figured the reason why we don't have a health care system that works and treats it as a basic right is not because it doesn't make the most sense or politicians don't understand how to make it work .... It's because there's not the right political pressure making them do it. So our strategy was just to show them that this is what we wanted over and over again" (as cited in McGill, 2012, p. 109).

The campaign's success was based upon its ability to engage Vermont residents in a variety of locales using multiple strategies. It relied upon volunteers to staff information tables at grocery stories, farmers' markets, participate in local parades and write letters to the editor in local newspapers. The VWC created relationships with unions, religious communities, businesses, and health care reform groups and received endorsements from influential organizations such as Vermont Health Care for All and the Vermont Nurses' Union. They crafted a "People's Toolkit" to use in public education and outreach. McGill (2012) notes that one of the most influential tactics was hosting state-wide human rights hearings and, later in the campaign, public forums. In public hearings and "People's Forums," community members provided testimony to local leaders, including legislators, about challenges they faced in accessing affordable and quality health care. The campaign also compiled some 1,500 surveys in which respondents provided personal stories about their challenges in accessing health care. Such stories, when shared in a 2008 report to elected officials, "humanized the health care crisis and helped ... explain the connection between human rights principles and the suffering of individual residents" (2012, p. 110). Once legislation was introduced in 2010, a "People's Team" of volunteers were active at the state legislature, attending all hearings related to health care legislation. Through these efforts, they were able to show broad-based support for the campaign, even as they fostered capacity among local residents to participate in political advocacy. In one innovation, organizers developed a series of questions to analyze three health care bills that had been introduced on the basis of how well each proposal met human rights standards (see Class Exercises and Additional Resources).

In 2010, the proposed legislation (H.100/S.88) was passed by both the Vermont House and Senate and became law. Notably, Act 128 (2010) does not say explicitly that there is a human right to health care. However, the law uses all the major human rights principles outlined in the UN Committee on Economic and Social

Right's General Comment No. 14 (2000). This is immediately apparent when examining the language of the legislation: It is "the policy of the state of Vermont to ensure *universal access* to and coverage for essential health services for all Vermonters. All Vermonters must have access to comprehensive, quality health care. Systemic barriers must not prevent people from accessing necessary health care" (section Defining the Right to Health and Health Care: International Standards and Practices). Moreover, "The health care system must be *transparent* in design, efficient in operation, and *accountable* to the people it serves. The state must ensure public *participation* in the design, implementation, evaluation, and *accountability* mechanisms in the health care system" (section Core Principles of the Right to Health and Health Care).

The passage of Act 128 was just the first step in the campaign to realize universal health care in Vermont. A second Bill, H.202, was introduced and passed in 2011 as Act 48. It "creates a framework for implementing a comprehensive, publicly financed universal health care system" called Green Mountain Care (McGill, 2012, p. 112). At the time of writing, Vermont is seeking to be exempted from federal requirements that would challenge the state's abilities to implement a publicly financed universal health care system. The case remains exemplary in terms of its achievements and potential, but the law has yet to be implemented. Notably, the Vermont model of organizing for health care reform at the state level has been so successful that other states such as Maryland and Maine have initiated similar campaigns. The fact that these efforts are expanding, even in the wake of the enactment of the federal law on health care reform, illustrates that access to health care remains a fundamental public concern.

Grassroots Mobilization—Fostering Meaningful Participation

Fostering community participation has been a central aim of community practice since its inception in the United States. As Gamble and Weil (2010) note, community may be defined by geographic locale or by those who share a common interest or goals but live and work in varied locations. They note that the principle that undergirds community organizing "derives from the democratic value that emphasizes how important it is that people be involved in decisions affecting their lives" (2010, p. 11). While human rights campaigning for justice both globally and in the United States has frequently relied upon "grassroots mobilization," fostering participation of groups whose economic and social rights have not been fulfilled is still in its early stages. Often the focus on human rights mobilization has been on civil and political rights violations (Becker, 2013). Efforts to articulate and demonstrate community involvement in campaigning for economic and social rights, as well as implementing and monitoring progress on achieving such rights, merit greater attention.

The model advanced by the National Economic and Social Rights Initiative (NESRI) in New York City is promising for rights-based community practice in the

United States. NESRI partners with grassroots and local organizations such as the Vermont Workers' Center to help define community interests, develop campaign goals, collaborate in drafting legislation, and provide training on human rights law and practices. Though NESRI is little more than 10 years old, it has already partnered with numerous organizations on a variety of economic and social rights campaigns and is a key facilitator in the Vermont, Maryland, and Maine efforts to implement rights-based approaches to health care. Lawyers and health care practitioners increasingly acknowledge the importance of community mobilization as well. Tyler (2013), a lawyer and clinical professor in health sciences, argued that "case-by-case advocacy" will not realize a health and human rights agenda. "The ultimate goal is systems accountability and change. This will only come with lawyers and health care providers partnering with and empowering communities to enforce and articulate their rights as human rights" (p. 88). The role of the community-based social work practitioner is central to this process.

Among the lessons learned from these local efforts to introduce a human rights framework for health and health care is that broad participation is vital to the success of shifting public discourse. This empowerment approach to participation seeks to mobilize community members for involvement in decision making, planning, implementation, and monitoring and evaluating health programming. Health practitioners have underscored that the participation process itself is important. But the more fundamental aims are to redistribute "resources and power in the political process" and increase the "ability of marginalized communities to control key processes that influence their lives" (De Vos, De Ceukelaire, Malaise, Pérez, Lefèvre, & Van der Stuyft, 2009, p. 25). It is too early to assess whether or not the Vermont campaign to realize universal health care defined in terms of human rights will result in such redistribution of resources and more equitable health outcomes. But the tools for such evaluation already have been defined by groups like the Vermont Workers' Center. Community social work practitioners should play important roles in assessing progress under the new legislation as a model to be considered in other parts of the United States.

Class Exercises and Additional Resources

For Discussion: The Core Minimum Obligations to the Right to Health in the US Context

According to the UN Committee on Economic, Social, and Cultural Rights, the core minimum obligations to the right to health include:

(a) "[A]ccess to health facilities, goods and services *on a non-discriminatory basis*, especially for vulnerable or marginalized groups";
(b) "Access to the *minimal essential food* which is nutritiously adequate and safe";

(c) "Access to *shelter, housing and sanitation* and an adequate supply of safe drinking water";
(d) "The provision of *essential drugs*"; and
(e) "*Equitable distribution* of all health facilities, goods and services"

(WHO, 2008, pp. 24–25).

Questions for Discussion

- Which of the core minimum obligations to the right to health exist in your community?
- Which of these core minimum obligations to the right to health would you prioritize in your community and why?
- What are the benefits and/or limitations of using a rights-based approach to health and health care in advocacy efforts?

For Discussion: Illustrating the Interdependence of Human Rights Through the Child's Right to Health and Health Care

Read the excerpt from a recent general comment of the Committee on the Rights of the Child (2013) concerning the child's right to the highest attainable standard of health. In small groups discuss the questions below.

> 28. Article 24, paragraph 1, imposes a strong duty of action by States parties to ensure that health and other relevant services are available and accessible to all children, with special attention to under-served areas and populations. It requires a comprehensive primary health-care system, an adequate legal framework and sustained attention to the underlying determinants of children's health.
>
> 29. Barriers to children's access to health services, including financial, institutional and cultural barriers, should be identified and eliminated. Universal free birth registration is a prerequisite and social protection interventions, including social security such as child grants or subsidies, cash transfers and paid parental leave, should be implemented and seen as complementary investments.

Questions for Discussion

- Have the barriers to children's access to health services (identified above) been eliminated in your community?
- How would you frame the issue of children's access to health care to generate public support to realize children's right to health and health care?
- What groups in your community and professional organizations (state, local) should be involved in efforts to address this human rights concern?

For Discussion: Does the United States Need a Constitutional Amendment on the Right to Health?

Over the past decade a number of Congressional representatives have introduced a proposed amendment to the US Constitution that would provide an entitlement to health care. Read the text of the proposed amendment introduced by Rep. Jesse Jackson, Jr. to the 108th Congress. Then discuss the questions that follow.

HJ 30 IH

108th CONGRESS

1st Session

H. J. RES. 30

Proposing an amendment to the Constitution of the United States regarding the right of citizens of the United States to health care of equal high quality.

IN THE HOUSE OF REPRESENTATIVES

March 4, 2003

Mr. JACKSON of Illinois introduced the following joint resolution; which was referred to the Committee on the Judiciary

---

JOINT RESOLUTION

Proposing an amendment to the Constitution of the United States regarding the right of citizens of the United States to health care of equal high quality.

Resolved by the Senate and House of Representatives of the United States of America in Congress assembled (two-thirds of each House concurring therein), That the following article is proposed as an amendment to the Constitution of the United States, which shall be valid to all intents and purposes as part of the Constitution when ratified by the legislatures of three-fourths of the several States:

'Article--

'SECTION 1. All citizens of the United States shall enjoy the right to health care of equal high quality.

'SECTION 2. The Congress shall have power to implement this article by appropriate legislation.'.

Questions for Discussion

- How would a federal Constitutional Amendment help advance a right to health care?
- What actions could lead to the adoption of such an amendment?
- What short-term and mid-term goals would be necessary to develop a campaign to amend the Constitution for a right to health care?
- What other approaches to ensure the human right to health care would likely generate public support?

Human Rights-Based Guidelines for Analyzing Vermont's Legislation

The following questions were used to analyze the state of Vermont's proposed legislation on health care in the late 2000s. They were directly tied to human rights principles for health care. Consider how these questions could be used in advocacy for health care in your community.

- Does the system provide health care for all?
- Does the system provide equal access to comprehensive health care services?
- Does the system treat health care as a public good?
- Does the system eliminate barriers to use needed health care services?
- Is the system financed equitably?
- Do people pay for their health care on their ability to pay without regard to unrelated factors such as age, gender, employment, or health status?
- Does the system use money effectively and efficiently?
- Does the system allocate resources equitably, according to health needs?
- Does the system improve the quality of health care by rewarding providers who utilize best practices and provide excellent outcomes?
- Does the system enable meaningful community participation?
- Is the system accountable to the people it serves?

Sources Adapted from McGill (2012, p. 111); see also more detailed guidelines with links to specific aspects of the right to health care on the Vermont Workers' Center website at: http://www.workerscenter.org/sites/default/files/hchr_hsiao_assessment.pdf.

Organizations in the United States Using a Health and Human Rights Perspective

Listed Below are Organizations that Advocate for Access to Health Care from a Human Rights Framework

- Healthcare is a Human Right: Accessible healing for all: http://healthcareisa-humanright.com/
- Healthcare NOW! Organizing for a National Single-Payer Healthcare System: http://www.healthcare-now.org/
- Montana Human Rights Network: http://www.mhrn.org
- National Economic and Social Rights Initiative: http://www.nesri.org/
- National Health Law Program: http://www.healthlaw.org/
- South L.A. Coalition for Health and Human Rights: http://www.southlahealthand-humanrights.org/about.html
- Vermont Workers Center-Healthcare is a Human Right Campaign: http://www.workerscenter.org/healthcare

Chapter 3
More Than a Commodity: The Right to Adequate Housing

> *The US does not support the "right to adequate housing" or "housing rights," because such a right does not exist.*
>
> —Ameri (as cited in International Women's Human Rights Clinic, City University of New York School of Law, 2009, p. 1)

> Access to adequate housing directly affects other human rights. Without it, employment is difficult to secure and maintain, health is threatened, education is impeded, violence is more easily perpetrated, privacy is impaired, and social relationships are frequently strained. The lack of affordable housing especially places poor people in the impossible position of having to choose between the most basic of human necessities: housing or food, housing or health care, housing or clothing, and so on. While many people think that violations of housing rights only occur amidst the grinding poverty of the developing world, the truth is that we do not have to go far to witness the housing crisis in our own cities and towns. (Gomez & Thiele, 2005)

The ideas expressed by Goli Ameri, a US delegate to the 61st Session of the UN Commission on Human Rights in 2005, starkly contrast with sentiments by housing rights advocates Myra Gomez and Brett Thiele. The two quotes underscore the polarization of views on housing as a human right. Indeed, the failure of the public sector—government—to guarantee access to safe and affordable housing has exacerbated a housing crisis perpetuated by private, market forces. Housing is one of the most complex and entrenched human rights concerns in the United States. In 1949, Congress passed the Housing Act (Title V of P.L. 81–171), declaring the *goal* that "every American family be able to afford a decent home in a suitable environment" (United States Department of Housing and Urban Development, n.d.). Yet since then, US housing policy has privileged supports for the private housing market, offering federal financing to mortgage lenders and tax breaks for home owners, and prioritized housing development meeting the needs of middle-class consumers. For millions of low- or moderate-income families, these trends have largely ignored their needs and contributed to a chronic affordable housing crisis. As a result, the policy goal articulated 65 years ago is a distant prospect for

K.R. Libal and S. Harding, *Human Rights-Based Community Practice in the United States*, SpringerBriefs in Rights-Based Approaches to Social Work,
DOI 10.1007/978-3-319-08210-3_3

many. Housing advocates have long argued that a shift is necessary—at local, state, and national levels—to ensure an obligation by government to secure housing that is decent, affordable, and universally available.

The fact that high rates of housing insecurity and homelessness persist in one of the wealthiest countries in the world reflects long-standing political and policy failures. Steep cuts in spending on public housing and low-income housing subsidies have occurred since the 1980s, while homeowner subsidies have expanded (National Economic and Social Rights Initiative, 2011). At the same time, homelessness has persisted and those with "worst-case housing needs" have steadily increased (Center on Budget and Policy Priorities, 2013a). The lack of affordable (rental) housing for low-income groups, defined as spending no more than 30 % of household income for shelter, has been exacerbated by policy decisions that privilege homeownership. Rental evictions and housing foreclosures have accelerated in the past 10 years, fueled by a weak economy and reduction of other forms of public assistance for low-income households. In a climate of increasing housing insecurity, local municipalities and governments have often responded to homelessness with punitive measures that are now broadly categorized as the "criminalization of homelessness" and poverty (Biron, 2014; National Law Center on Homelessness and Poverty, 2011a).

Like claims to health and food, recognizing housing as a human right in the United States is contested. This chapter outlines a nascent movement to assure decent and affordable housing from a human rights perspective. Community organizations and legal advocacy groups are increasingly using human rights standards and monitoring processes to help reframe access to housing. One of the most visible expressions of this interest occurred in the 2009 mission of the United Nations Special Rapporteur on adequate housing as a component of the right to an adequate standard of living, and on the right to non-discrimination in this context (hereafter the Special Rapporteur on the Right to Adequate Housing). The Rapporteur, Raquel Rolnik, was invited by the Obama administration to the United States to investigate claims by housing advocates that decent, affordable housing was out of reach for millions of families. She visited with community organizations and gathered insights from residents, local agencies, and members of government in Washington D.C., New York, Chicago, New Orleans, the Pine Ridge (Indian) Reservation, Los Angeles, and Pacoima (California).

In her report to the UN Human Rights Council, Rolnik found that the majority of housing in the United States was high quality and that utilities and services for most people met human rights standards. But she also expressed "deep concern about the millions of people living in the United States today who face serious challenges in accessing affordable and adequate housing, issues long faced by the poorest people and today affecting a greater proportion of society" (UN Special Rapporteur on the Right to Adequate Housing, 2010, paragraph 79). The Rapporteur recommended that the United States:

- Provide more funding for federal housing programs for low-income households (including more funds for affordable housing vouchers);
- Prioritize the maintenance and restoration of the public housing stock;
- Refrain from forcing families out of communities where public housing is being redeveloped;
- Develop measures to prevent housing foreclosures; and
- Develop alternatives to the growing practice of criminalizing homelessness.

Understanding how each of these circumstances constitutes a human rights issue is an important step for community practitioners. In this chapter, we outline what a human right to adequate housing means in international law, define current US obligations to secure this right, and address the role of community practice in transforming ideas about housing as a human right. The National Association of Social Workers Delegate Assembly has asserted in its most recent policy statement on housing that all individuals and families have a right to "affordable housing that meets their basic needs for shelter and provides for a rewarding community life" (2012, p. 195). This chapter seeks to highlight ways that community-based social workers can participate in the realization of such a right.

Defining the Right to Housing: International Standards and Practices

The right to housing was first expressed in Article 25 of the Universal Declaration of Human Rights (United Nations, 1948), as part of the host of economic and social rights that corresponded to the right to an adequate standard of living. The International Covenant on Economic, Social, and Cultural Rights (United Nations, 1966) elaborates in Article 11(1): "The State parties to the present Covenant recognize the right of everyone to an adequate standard of living for himself [or herself] and for his [or her] family, including adequate food, clothing and housing, and to the continuous improvement of living conditions." The UN Committee on Economic, Social, and Cultural Rights recognizes the right to adequate housing as a freestanding right and has most fully articulated its meaning in General Comments No. 4 (1991) and No. 7 (1997). Other human rights treaties also address housing either directly or indirectly, though the right to housing in the United States has largely involved government obligations to refrain from discriminating against minority groups in its housing policies and practices. Advocates have used both the standards for non-discrimination under the International Convention on the Elimination of All Forms of Racial Discrimination and the International Covenant on Civil and Political Rights (ICCPR) to advance housing rights claims (National Law Center on Homelessness and Poverty, 2011a; 2014a; 2014b). Housing rights advocates have also used the Human Rights Council Universal Periodic Review process and monitoring mechanisms under the UN Convention Against Torture and Other Cruel, Inhuman or Degrading Treatment and Punishment to press human rights claims (National Law Center on Homelessness and Poverty and The US Human Rights Network UPR Housing Working Group, 2014; National Law Center on Homelessness and Poverty, 2014b). While the connections between civil and political rights and the right to housing may not be immediately obvious, the Human Rights Committee which monitors the ICCPR found in the late 1990s that the right to housing was inherently linked to the right to life (Article 6). In the case of Canada, for example, the Human Rights Committee expressed concern that homelessness undermined health and in some instances arbitrarily deprived individuals of their lives (UN Human Rights Committee, 1999, paragraph 12). The Human Rights Committee recently asserted that the United States must "abolish the laws criminalizing homelessness at state and local levels," citing concerns about "discrimination and cruel, inhuman, or degrading treatment" (UN Human Rights Committee, 2014, paragraph 19).

Though the right to housing has largely been defined by the Committee on Economic, Social, and Cultural Rights, in recent years, the Special Rapporteur on the Right to Adequate Housing, operating under the authority of the UN Human Rights Council, also has provided important insight into this issue. In the US case, the Rapporteur is an important authority, given that the United States has not ratified the ICESCR and thus does not submit regular reports to the United Nations. Similarly, since 2010, the Human Rights Council's Universal Periodic Review process, in which the United States is reviewed on its human rights record every 4 years, has been an important forum in which human rights groups and advocates have been able to raise questions of the right to housing (National Law Center on Homelessness and Poverty and The US Human Rights Network UPR Housing Working Group, 2014).

Core Principles of the Right to Housing

The core principles of the right to housing are similar to the right to health and health care: As an economic right, it is to be *progressively realized*, primarily by the government providing a legislative and policy context for securing adequate housing for all people. Two general comments on the right to adequate housing and the work of the special rapporteur provide greater insights into the parameters of the right and guidelines for advocacy and implementation.

The Committee on Economic, Social, and Cultural Rights finalized General Comment No. 4 on the right to adequate housing in 1991. In this document, the Committee underscored that the right to housing should not be interpreted as a right to "shelter provided by merely having a roof over one's head," nor should housing be understood "exclusively as a commodity" (1991, paragraph 7). Instead, the Committee stated that the right to housing "should be seen as the right to live somewhere in security, peace and dignity" (paragraph 7). The Committee has also identified the connection between housing and community and the interrelationship of these domains for human dignity.

The Committee on Economic, Social, and Cultural Rights (1991) has defined the right to *adequate* housing as including seven core elements:

1. *Security of tenure*: Residents "should possess a degree of security of tenure which guarantees legal protection against forced eviction, harassment and other threats," including predatory redevelopment and displacement (paragraph 8a);
2. *Availability of services, materials, facilities, and infrastructure*: An "adequate house must contain certain facilities essential for health, security, comfort and nutrition," and beneficiaries "should have sustainable access to natural and common resources, safe drinking water, energy for cooking, heating and lighting, sanitation and washing facilities, means of food storage, refuse disposal, site drainage and emergency services" (paragraph 8b);
3. *Affordability*: Financial costs of housing should not undermine the "attainment and satisfaction of other basic needs," and governments must take steps to "ensure that the percentage of housing-related costs is, in general, commensurate with income levels," establishing "housing subsidies for those unable to obtain affordable housing, as well as forms and levels of housing finance which adequately reflect housing needs" (paragraph 8c);
4. *Habitability*: Adequate housing must be habitable, providing "adequate space and protecting them from cold, damp, heat, rain, wind or other threats to health, structural hazards, and disease vectors" as well as guaranteeing the "physical safety of occupants" (paragraph 8d);
5. *Accessibility*: Disadvantaged groups such as the elderly, children, physically disabled, terminally ill, HIV-positive individuals, mentally ill, and victims of natural disasters "should be ensured some degree of priority consideration" in housing and "housing law and policy should take fully into account the special housing needs of these groups" (paragraph 8e);
6. *Location*: The location of housing in rural, suburban, and urban areas must allow access to employment options, health care services, schools, and child care facilities; housing "should not be built on polluted sites nor in immediate proximity to pollution sources that threaten the right to health of the inhabitants" (paragraph 8f);
7. *Cultural adequacy*: "The way housing is constructed, the building materials used and the policies supporting these must appropriately enable the expression of cultural identity and diversity of housing" (paragraph 8g).

The right to adequate housing, like health care, entails government obligations to *respect*, *protect*, and *fulfill* the right. Government *respect* for the right to adequate housing applies to a number of concerns, including respecting the right to freedom of assembly and expression regarding housing policy and practices; abstaining from forced or arbitrary evictions of residents without due process; and observing equality of treatment and privacy in the home. *Protecting* the right to housing entails protecting residents from "third-party" actors, such as landlords and private developers, from forced or arbitrary eviction; housing discrimination; or unsafe housing conditions. This also requires a legal mechanism for redress when rights are violated. *Fulfilling* the right to adequate housing addresses the positive legislative and policy action needed to secure the right to adequate housing. It addresses "public expenditure, government regulation of the economy and land market, the provision of public services and related infrastructure, the redistribution of income [taxation], and other positive obligations" (National Law Center on Homelessness and Poverty, 2011b, p. 38).

The Committee allows for a wide variety of policy and legal approaches to realize the right to housing, including market regulation, subsidies, public–private partnerships, tax policies, and public housing. The obligation to fulfill the right to adequate housing is based on the principle that this right should be *progressively realized* based on the maximum use of available resources. As the National Law Center on Homelessness and Poverty (2011b) underscores, "Implementing the human right to housing would not require the government to immediately build a home for each person in America or to provide housing for all free of charge. But it does require more than some provision for emergency shelter—it requires an affirmative commitment to ensure fully adequate housing" (p. 22).

Moreover, the right to housing is recognized as integral and related to other human rights, including civil and political rights. This is particularly relevant in the United States, which has ratified the International Covenant on Civil and Political Rights. The Committee on Economic, Social, and Cultural Rights claims that "the full enjoyment of other rights—such as the right to freedom of expression, the right to freedom of association (for tenants and other community-based groups), the right to freedom of residence and the right to participate in public decision-making—is indispensable if the right to adequate housing is to be realized and maintained by all groups in society" (1991, paragraph 9). Further, "the right not to be subjected to arbitrary or unlawful interference with one's privacy, family, home or correspondence" is also crucial to defining the right to adequate housing.

U.S. Obligations for Securing the Right to Housing

Despite passage of several national housing acts (dating to 1934) and the existence of numerous federal housing programs, US housing policy is marked by its fragmented nature. According to Maria Foscarinis, Executive Director of the National Law Center on Homelessness and Poverty (NLCHP), "The U.S. has a patchwork of laws addressing housing needs, but there is no right defined and the resources provided through existing law are by far inadequate to the need" (National Law Center on Homelessness and Poverty, 2011b, p. 17). Of significance, this piecemeal approach remains embedded within a framework that privileges the private housing market. National housing policy is thus marked by both an imbalance toward promoting homeownership and attempts at social engineering to address the limitations of the private sector. Despite sizeable expenditures on housing programs and an intricate national network of housing providers and advocates, this effort has largely failed to solve several long-standing problems:

- Persistent racial segregation in the housing market;
- The lack of affordable housing and access to safe and decent housing, especially for millions of low- and moderate-income households;
- The continued existence of a sizeable population experiencing homelessness.

To be sure, significant progress has been made since the formulation of a federal housing policy. Record levels of homeownership, declining racial discrimination in the housing market through a focus on "fair housing" law, an expanded public housing market and rental subsidies, and creation of effective programs (like "supportive housing") to serve some of the homeless population all suggest progress toward housing for all people. But the inability to guarantee a right to housing —a foundation of social inclusion in any society—continues to leave large segments of US society vulnerable to the whims of the free market status quo.

In 2011, more than eight million American families suffered "worst-case housing needs," a nearly 50 % increase since 2007 and the start of the Great Recession. These families paid more than half of their income for rent or lived in severely inadequate housing (Center on Budget and Policy Priorities, 2013a; Urban Institute, 2014). In addition, nearly 22 million households were "doubled-up" (living with family or friends), a further reflection of the extent of housing instability in the United States (Urban Institute, 2014).

In contrast, a notable decline in homelessness began in 2007, due largely to the adoption of a "Housing First" model to address those lacking a permanent residence (Urban Institute, 2014). Under the federal "Opening Doors" model, resources have increasingly targeted those at significant risk of homelessness: veterans, persons with disabilities with a recent history of homelessness, and the chronically homeless. Based on best practices in local communities, Housing First "prioritizes immediate placement into permanent housing instead of making housing contingent upon substance abuse treatment, sobriety, or other milestones" and "has emerged as a best practice for ending homelessness for even the hardest cases" (Leopold, 2014, n.p.).

Despite this policy success, there is a continued need to target resources for those at risk of/experiencing homelessness—especially families—given the lack of rental assistance and the shortage of affordable housing for low-income households. More American families spend at least 30 % of annual income on housing than do those with "worst-case" housing needs. In 2012, more than half of US renters spent in excess of 30 % of their gross income on rent, exceeding the government's measure of housing affordability (Maciag, 2013). Large numbers of homeowners with a mortgage also face housing burdens: Approximately one-third claim housing-related expenses in excess of 30 % of income. Still, the problem of affordability is most severe for renters, a group that typically earns less than homeowners (Maciag, 2013).

The Joint Center for Housing Studies of Harvard University (2013) found that the lack of affordable rental housing in part reflects a shortage of housing supply given growing demand. Rising home foreclosures and wage stagnation, especially for younger workers, has increased the pool of renters nationwide. In turn, greater demand fueled higher rental costs as vacancy rates fell across the United States since the mid-2000s. Between 2000 and 2012, median rent increased 6 %, while renters' median incomes plummeted 13 % (adjusted for inflation). Not surprisingly, low-income households were more likely to be cost-burdened (rent in excess of 30 % of income) or severely cost-burdened (rent in excess of 50 % of income). "An astounding 83 % of renters with incomes of less than $15,000 were housing cost burdened in 2011, including a dismal 71 % with severe burdens" (Joint Center for Housing Studies, 2013, p. 6). Supporting other studies, researchers found that the (rental) affordability problem largely stems from a severe shortage of housing for low- and moderate-income households.

> Consider the case of renters with $15,000 in annual income. To meet the 30-percent-of-income affordability standard, they would have to find housing that costs no more than $375 a month. By comparison, the 2011 median monthly cost for housing built within the previous four years was more than $1,000. Less than 34 % of these new units rented for less than $800, and only 5 % for less than $400. Given this mismatch, it is no surprise that the gap between the number of lower-income renters and the supply of affordable units continues to grow. (Joint Center for Housing Studies, 2013, p. 6)

As housing advocates emphasize, the United States already is obliged to address housing as a human right under current treaty commitments. Yet in 2005, Ameri Goli, the US representative to the UN Commission on Human Rights openly rejected the notion that a right to housing existed, which was consonant with other positions taken by then President George W. Bush (International Women's Right Clinic, CUNY Law, 2009). Advocates have subsequently used treaty monitoring processes for the Convention on the Elimination of All Forms of Racial Discrimination and the Covenant on Civil and Political Rights and the Universal Periodic Review process before the Human Rights Council to engage US officials in acknowledging basic housing rights. Since President Obama was elected in 2008, the US government has been more open to discussing core aspects of the right to housing. For example, in 2011, after the UN review of its human rights compliance under the UPR process, the US government acknowledged a UN recommendation that it continues to address access to housing "vital for the realization of several other rights … in order to meet the needs for adequate housing at an affordable price for all" (United Nations Human Rights Council, 2010, paragraph 92.197; United States Department of State, 2011).

Recently, activists have addressed the criminalization of homelessness as a civil rights concern—one that at its very core is about the right to life. The criminalization of homelessness includes actions such as making it illegal to sleep or sit in public spaces when adequate shelter or housing is not available; sweeps of cities to drive out homeless individuals; destruction of homeless individuals' belongings; restrictions on sharing food in public spaces; and enforcement of panhandling ordinances as a means to force homeless individuals to leave a community. The National Law Center on Homeless and Poverty (NLCHP) has led efforts to work with grassroots and national non-governmental organizations to incorporate human rights principles and practices in their work. NLCHP has also been a leader in facilitating dialogue between the United Nations and US government agencies and advocacy groups. A core aspect of their work has been to highlight the US government's failure to respect, protect, and fulfill the right to adequate housing. They have focused on the criminalization of homelessness as a growing and troubling example of violating the most basic premises of human rights (National Law Center on Homelessness and Poverty, 2011a; 2014a; 2014b).

At a state level, the use of human rights framing is even more apparent, to combat the criminalization of homelessness, housing foreclosures and evictions, reduction of public housing stock, and neighborhood redevelopment without providing affordable alternatives for low-income residents (Dahmann & Dennison, 2013; Gardiner, Irwin, & Peterson, 2009). Prominent examples of human rights principles in community practice on the issue of affordable housing can be seen in Chicago, Los Angeles, and New Orleans.

Overview of Housing Policies

Since enactment of the first National Housing Act (1934) and the Wagner-Steagall Housing Act (1937), efforts to meet housing needs in the United States have largely been the responsibility of the federal government. Over time, states and localities have also sought to address the lack of affordable housing and homelessness, though the bulk of housing resources continue to generate from Washington D.C. While stereotypes persist of a vast network of subsidized housing for "welfare" recipients and others in poverty, in fact, initiatives to promote private homeownership have been prioritized for decades. Yet as noted, low-income households—primarily renters—typically experience greater housing burdens than homeowners. Despite this disparity, vital programs do exist to reduce homelessness and provide aid to large numbers of tenuously housed Americans.

Rental Assistance

Federal assistance serves more than 10 million people in low-income rental households. Most of these families utilize three programs: the Housing Choice Vouchers program, Section 8 Project-based Rental Assistance, and public housing, while other programs serve the elderly, persons with HIV/AIDS, and persons with disabilities. Adults with children, the elderly, and disabled adults comprise more than 80 % of those assisted. On a smaller scale, funding for new construction and rehabilitation of low- and moderate-income rental housing also exists, though rental subsidies are often needed to ensure that such housing is affordable to the poorest families (Center on Budget and Policy Priorities, 2013a). Through these initiatives, eligible households must have a "low income" that is no more than 80 % of the local median income. Families typically pay 30 % of their income on rent, and the rental assistance subsidy reimburses the remaining cost (Center on Budget and Policy Priorities, 2013a).

The *Housing Choice Vouchers* program, the largest federal rental subsidy, was created in 1974 as part of the Housing and Community Development Act. It serves more than five million people in two million low-income families. Eligible households use a "voucher" to help pay for private-market rental housing through a network of state and local housing agencies (Center on Budget and Policy Priorities, 2013b). Most vouchers target "extremely low-income" households (incomes below 30 % of local median income), with other households eligible if their income is no more than 80 % of local median income. Families that receive a voucher have two months to find private housing or use their voucher for their current housing; in either case, a local housing agency must certify the unit meets federal standards.

The *Section 8 Project-based Rental Assistance* program serves more than two million low-income households, mostly elderly individuals and persons with disabilities. Eligible households—with incomes up to 80 % of local median income—live in housing where some or all units are designated as "low income." At least 40 % of units serve "extremely low-income" households with incomes below 30 % of local median income, while most others serve those with income up to 50 % of local median income. Private owners, who contract with local housing agencies or the federal government through multi-year agreements, manage housing.

More than 2 million low-income people live in 1.1 million *Public Housing* units. Public housing is federally financed and administered locally through public housing agencies, which own and manage these units (sometimes using private management companies). Much of the nation's public housing stock was built prior to 1985, resulting in an aging infrastructure with a vast backlog of unmet renovation needs. In addition,

> [n]o funds have been provided to build additional public housing since the mid-1990s. Since then, housing agencies have demolished or otherwise removed from the program more than 260,000 units due to deterioration resulting from long-term underfunding and other factors. Agencies have built new units to replace only about one-sixth of those that have been removed. (Center on Budget and Policy Priorities, 2013b)

These different subsidies serve their stated purpose: assisting low-income families obtain affordable and stable rental housing. They may also help reduce homelessness. Fischer (2013), for example, found that a part of the Housing Choice Vouchers program that serves veterans had a significant impact in reducing homelessness among veterans between 2009 and 2013.

However, as has been the case for decades, the lack of adequate funding for "public housing" programs means that a majority of qualified families fail to receive housing subsidies: Nationally, only one in four eligible low-income households receive rental assistance (Center on Budget and Policy Priorities, 2013d). In addition, most public housing agencies have long waiting lists that often contain the names of thousands of families. Thus, many eligible families must wait years before accessing subsidized housing, while others are unable to have their names accepted, as local housing agencies have "closed" their lists to new families. As a result, millions of renter households spend well in excess of 30 % of their income on housing; many more low-income families are precariously housed, and the risk and actual incidence of homelessness is significantly increased among this population.

Homeownership

Compared to rental assistance programs, the federal government spends nearly three times as much each year on subsidies for homeownership, "more than half of which benefits households with incomes above $100,000" (Center on Budget and Policy Priorities, 2013a). Through a number of policy mechanisms, government actively supports and subsidizes private homeownership. Whether seeking to create more "stable" neighborhoods, to provide a means for individual wealth creation, or simply to support the private sector, public involvement in housing expanded dramatically since the 1930s. Over time, these efforts have far surpassed support for those unable to purchase their own home, especially low-income households and those with significant "housing burdens."

Homeowners are eligible to receive a tax refund on their house up to its first one million dollars in value (as are those owning a second home). Those who itemize their taxes may reduce their annual tax burden by deducting the amount of interest they pay on their home mortgage from their taxable income—the so-called mortgage interest deduction. As a result, most homeowners receive some tax rebate each year, the value of which increases based on household income. Thus, since wealthier households are able to afford more expensive homes, there is an inverse relationship in the distribution of the subsidy: The bigger, more expensive the house (and higher household income), the bigger the tax credit one receives. Other tax "incentives" exist for homeowners and property owners that totaled more than $200 billion in government subsidies in 2012.

Government support for homeownership was largely denied for African-Americans and other racial minorities through different efforts, both formal and informal, that existed until the 1970s. At the same time, local lending and real estate practices reinforced residential segregation and prevented most racial minorities from the psychological and financial benefits associated with homeownership (Segrue, 1996; Jackson, 1985; Massey & Denton, 1993). As a result of race-specific housing policy and private practices, racial identity and concepts of whiteness emerged as key phenomenon in post-war America. Writing about the case of Chicago (but noting similarities to other US cities), Hirsch (1998) describes how such housing initiatives strengthened racial and class difference and helped "create" distinct racial ghettos. The legacy of such efforts continues to haunt the US housing market: Racial minorities own homes at lower rates than whites, on average their houses are worth less than whites, and in general, they have less accrued equity in their homes than white homeowners. During the recent housing crisis, non-white homeowners had much higher rates of foreclosure than whites. In addition, most American communities remain marked by racial (and class) segregation.

Homelessness

The 1987 McKinney-Vento Act was the first federal legislation designed to deal with what had become a growing national problem of homelessness. Then, as now, private efforts—including reliance on charities, family, and friends—were seen as a practical response to the loss of housing. McKinney-Vento was significant in that it formalized a primary role for government in seeking to alleviate the conditions of homelessness. Over time, in conjunction with federal housing initiatives, various policies have also sought to *prevent* individuals from becoming homeless.

Several programs comprise the current federal response to a lack of permanent housing. These include the emergency shelter grant (ESG) and the Continuum of Care, which combined three supportive and transitional housing programs, as well as funds for rental subsidies and housing rehabilitation. The 2009 Homeless Emergency Assistance and Rapid Transition to Housing (HEARTH) Act reauthorized federal homeless assistance programs and marked a formal policy shift to focus on the prevention of homelessness and chronic homelessness, and promote the "rapid re-housing" and permanent housing of homeless individuals. The HEARTH Act also formalized the Continuum of Care planning process, an effort to provide "wrap-around" services and increased coordination among homeless service providers, while promoting greater flexibility in homeless services (National Alliance to End Homelessness, 2009).

In 2010, the US Interagency Council on Homelessness announced concrete goals to end chronic homelessness. These were outlined in *Opening Doors*: *Federal Strategic Plan to Prevent and End Homelessness* (US Interagency Council on Homelessness, 2010), expressing the intent to end homelessness among veterans in 5 years and for families, children, and youth in 10 years. The report noted the interrelationship between housing stability and health outcomes for homeless individuals. The Council also underscored the need for constructive approaches to addressing a lack of shelter that do not criminalize homeless individuals. Starting in late 2013, in part through the advocacy of groups like the NLCHP, the Council began to use human rights-based standards in its policy discussions (United States Interagency Council on Homelessness, n.d.; Tars, 2014.

Federal programs have increased the number of homeless people who utilize emergency shelters or transitional housing programs, rather than sleeping in unsheltered conditions. States and localities have also devised programs designed to assist low-income families staying in homeless shelters, facing a housing crisis, or at risk of homelessness to remain in their existing housing, identify new housing, and/or address household financial crises that threaten their housing stability. In some cases, this has involved the use of federal temporary assistance to needy families (TANF) funds (Schott, 2010) or a special deduction in the Supplemental Nutrition Assistance Program (SNAP) program that allows homeless families to receive all their eligible benefits (Jones, 2011). Recent amendments to the McKinney-Vento Act seek to ensure that homeless youth are provided access to school no matter where they are housed. Changes to the Violence Against Women

Act in 2006 prevent women in public/subsidized housing from being evicted based on the behavior of their abuser and allow survivors to be transferred to other subsidized housing (National Law Center on Homelessness and Poverty, n.d.-a). The 2009 Protecting Tenants at Foreclosure Act seeks to help tenants in foreclosed rental properties from immediate eviction (National Law Center on Homelessness and Poverty, n.d.-b).

While these policies to address housing needs are notable in their intent, they fail to fully meet human rights standards. Fundamentally, programs serving low-income families are underfunded and do not provide access to resources on a universal basis as an entitlement.

The Role of Community Practice in Securing the Right to Housing

The lack of affordable housing in the United States has been a chronic problem for decades. Despite the country's wealth and advancements in law and policy, housing insecurity and homelessness are entrenched. The right to housing is realized by individuals and families *within* community settings, and in the US case, a mix of local, state, and federal programs shape the neighborhood and community environment. In this context, the role of community practitioners, particularly as organizers, is critical for building awareness of human rights standards for housing. Organizers can support the work of public interest and human rights lawyers, inform policy-makers, and, most importantly, galvanize low-income communities to shape housing policies to address their needs. Human rights-based community practice includes community education on human rights; the identification of human rights violations at local, national, or global levels; and organizing to address failures to realize human rights (Pyles, 2006). Community practice to realize the human right to housing is thus an inherently *local endeavor*, predicated on fostering participation and inclusion (Dahmann & Dennison, 2013). In the following section, we highlight several successful, ongoing efforts to address housing from a human rights perspective.

Chicago/Cook County, Illinois

Chicago and Cook County, Illinois, have been a center of housing rights advocacy, whether understood as a civil rights issue in the 1950s–1990s or as a broader human rights concern more recently. Historically, a destination during the Great Migration of African-Americans from the South, Chicago, has been one of the most racially diverse cities in the northern United States (Hirsch, 1998). Access to adequate housing in Chicago has also long been linked to racial justice. The realities of racial segregation, redlining and steering practices in real estate, lower school funding based on property values in racially segregated neighborhoods, and the effects of post-1950s deindustrialization have influenced contemporary housing rights concerns. Efforts to dismantle public housing and replace it with a mixture of Housing Choice Vouchers and affordable rental units have been a focus of advocacy since the 1990s. Since the 1990s, the Chicago Housing Authority demolished 82 public housing projects and failed to provide replacement housing for former residents (Austen, 2013). At the same time, following the 2007 housing crisis, in which record numbers of individuals found their homes foreclosed due to predatory lending practices, housing vacancies have greatly increased in Chicago. It is in this context that resident mobilization to recognize housing as a human right has emerged.

Housing rights advocacy in Chicago is predicated on grassroots community organizing, with neighborhood groups and larger organizations working (often in coalition) to address issues of racial segregation, exclusionary lending practices, the degradation or destruction of public housing, and the lack of subsidies for rental assistance. Over the past two decades, local groups have increasingly cited the human right to adequate housing in their advocacy, including proposals for one-for-one replacement of public housing being destroyed to make way for new development; in efforts to combat discriminatory practices that exclude those with Section 8 or Housing Choice Vouchers from renting in inner city and suburban communities; and in combatting predatory lending practices and forced evictions and foreclosures.

The Chicago Anti-Eviction Campaign has gained national attention for its efforts to place low-income families in renovated, abandoned, or foreclosed houses in the wake of the post-2007 housing crisis (Terry, 2011). The Anti-Eviction Campaign is also taking place in several other US cities. Under the leadership of Willie J.R. Fleming and Touissaint Losier, since 2009 the Campaign has created a citywide Human Right to Housing Collective made up of Chicago Housing Authority tenants and families facing foreclosure. They have worked alongside another resident advocacy group, Occupy Our Homes, to identify abandoned and unoccupied property suitable to occupy (legally known as "squatting"). The groups have used an "exception in the Illinois trespass statute that exempts someone from prosecution if he or she enters an abandoned and unoccupied property and 'beautifies' it" (Austen, 2013). Utilizing a human rights model developed in Cape Town, South Africa, activists in the Anti-Eviction Campaign find abandoned properties, canvass door to door in the neighborhood to gain support for having a family occupy the identified unit, and then assist the family to rehabilitate the property. The Campaign also advocates to keep residents from being evicted from their homes in the first place, engaging local media, providing free legal assistance, and blockading evictions in direct action. These tactics have helped garner national media attention, as well as the focus of United Nations officials, who have investigated housing rights matters in the United States since 2009. As the Anti-Eviction Campaign spreads throughout the country, community practitioners may find themselves well positioned to facilitate local dialogue about the right to adequate housing.

Los Angeles, California

In preparation for the first official visit to the United States by the Special Rapporteur on the Right to Housing, several community organizations and legal advocates formed the Los Angeles Human Right to Housing Collective (Dahmann & Dennison, 2013). After the Rapporteur's 2009 visit, the Collective spent four months developing a human rights-based plan for coalition work and committed to "a core purpose to lead and to coordinate the preservation and improvement of public housing in communities" throughout Los Angeles (Dahmann & Dennison, 2013, p. 78). The Collective defines its mission as "to build a city wide tenants movement and create a network of resident-led organizations and committees that can build power to implement the principle of the human right to housing in LA housing policies" (Los Angeles Human Right to Housing Collective, n.d.).

The Collective identifies *community participation* and *inclusion* as core values. Only groups involved in community organizing as central to their practice are eligible as members. Currently, these include Communidad Presente, Los Angeles Community Action Network, Los Angeles Anti-Eviction Campaign, People Organized for Westside Renewal, Union de Vecinos, and the Legal Aid Foundation of Los Angeles (Los Angeles Human Right to Housing Collective, n.d.). Twelve other supporting groups, including the National Economic and Social Rights Initiative (NESRI) and NLCHP at the national level, inform the Collective's work. Since its inception, the Collective has sought to assure participation of impacted groups—in this instance public housing tenants—and to foster leadership through resident-led housing rights committees. After the Collective was formed, more than 500 members from several public housing units participated in LA Human Right to Housing organizations, and more than 100 became leaders and decision-makers in the organizing efforts (Dahmann & Dennison, 2013).

Active members in the Collective have helped to identify community priorities through regular meetings, outreach, and a community survey. As a result, the Collective "prioritized the improvement of community and individual health in communities across the city by promoting and defending the human right to housing" (2013, p. 79). The Collective directly engages the concepts of core components to the human right to housing outlined by the UN Committee on Economic and Social Rights in General Comment No. 4 (1991) and explicitly cites the interdependence and interrelatedness of the right to housing and health. Throughout its efforts, the Collective has identified several aspects of community health realized through public housing: "(1) long-term housing stability without fear of displacement; (2) healthy conditions within and around homes; access to park space, grocery stores and fresh foods; health and mental health care, and other health-promoting resources; and (3) strong neighborhood social ties reflected by participation in community organizing and other clubs, activities, and events" (Dahmann & Dennison, 2013, p. 79).

Since 2009, sustained community-based work has allowed the Collective to identify its priorities as public housing preservation and access to high-quality grocery stores and fresh food. As a measure of its impact, the Collective temporarily prevented privatization plans for public housing, secured improvements in maintenance efforts by the Housing Authority of the City of Los Angeles (HACLA), and facilitated tenant participation in HACLA. The Collective's future goals are to permanently halt plans to privatize public housing; improve public housing stock through capital investment; develop deeper participatory processes in HACLA, including participatory budgeting; foster partnerships to promote community health and access to parks, high-quality grocery stores, health care, and employment programs; and ally with other organizations to foster public housing preservation and community health (Dahmann & Dennison, 2013).

New Orleans, Louisiana

Hurricane Katrina, which struck New Orleans and the Gulf Coast region of the United States in August, 2005, has been a catalyst for human rights-based community organizing in the United States (Finger & Luft, 2011; Pyles, 2006). The outcomes of this organizing may seem limited in terms of rehabilitating and rebuilding public housing lost to the storm; local mobilization has not secured substantial new funding or even stopped the destruction of public housing. But, human rights-based strategies and tactics used by community members, many of whom were marginalized residents, often displaced for years from their homes and neighborhoods, have become models for mobilization in other US communities.

One analysis of the human rights implications of government failures in New Orleans cites the relationships between structural racism and human rights violations, including the right to adequate housing (Gardiner et al., 2009). The authors note that "Public authorities' failure to prepare adequately meant that poor, predominantly Black communities bore the brunt" of the hurricane (p. 101). They argue that post-Katrina recovery efforts have exacerbated discriminatory public policies, noting that at "the heart of human rights concerns plaguing the city's reconstruction lies the systematic violation of the right to housing for New Orleans' poor Black residents." Robert Tanner, a local housing advocate, asserts that policies adopted by the Housing Authority of New Orleans (HANO) and the US Department of Housing and Urban Development (HUD) have intentionally prevented the relocation of poor residents to their historic neighborhoods and housing: "After the disaster there was a desire for a clean slate on the part of local leaders…and that clean slate mostly displaces poor and minority residents" (as cited in Gardiner et al., 2009, p. 104).

In preparation for the 2009 visit of the UN Special Rapporteur on the Right to Adequate Housing to New Orleans, local community organizers compiled data outlining the radical drop in public housing stock post-Katrina. The "fact sheet" prepared for the Special Rapporteur highlighted a New Orleans City Council decision in 2007 to demolish the "Big Four" public housing complexes (B.W. Cooper, C.J. Peete, Lafitte, and St. Bernard). As a result, nearly 4,500 units were slated to be replaced with "mixed-income developments" (Campaign to Restore

National Housing Blog, 2012, October 29). According to advocates, redevelopment plans included only 750 units of public housing in new mixed-income developments. Moreover, new housing units were estimated to cost $400,000 each to build, while repairing units in the Big Four would cost only $10,000 each. Earlier that year, the new HUD Secretary, Shaun Donovan, met with private developers and other government officials, but denied requests to meet with public housing residents. As one blogger for the Campaign to Restore National Housing put it, "Donovan's actions violated one of the key components of the human right (sic) to housing and to development—community participation. According to human rights standards development must regard the opinion of community members as of equal value to those of analysts, academics, planners, and the private sector. Participation by community members must be meaningful, active and well integrated into development planning" (2012, May 11).

A number of grassroots organizations in New Orleans have embraced the right to participation in shaping local housing policy and practice. Public housing resident organizations such as Mayday New Orleans have partnered with national advocacy groups, such as the NESRI, the Center for Constitutional Rights, and the Poverty Initiative, to challenge public housing demolition plans and to realize "the right of residents to participate in decision-making" (National Economic and Social Rights Initiative, n.d). Seeking to foster equitable rebuilding of housing affected by Hurricane Katrina, NESRI and Mayday developed a housing survey to be implemented by trained residents of public housing. Conducting training to administer the survey with local housing resident volunteers provided an opportunity for public education and organizing. Survey findings were also incorporated into human rights reporting, helping to challenge post-Katrina efforts to gentrify or redevelop neighborhoods that had originally had a large proportion of public housing stock.

Capacity-Building and Fostering Participation for Housing Rights Advocacy

As the examples from Los Angeles and New Orleans illustrate, rights-based community practice is predicated on the fundamental idea of fostering meaningful participation and inclusion of community members who do not have stable and affordable housing. This is consistent with community organizing principles for achieving social justice. A human rights-based approach integrates specific standards and conceptualizations of the human right to housing. This framework requires residents and community groups to be centrally involved in change efforts. Thus, any community assessments or surveys of those residing in public housing, benefitting from rental assistance programs, or living in housing slated for "redevelopment," should include the participation of affected residents themselves. Human rights education on housing and interrelated rights also should be widely available within neighborhoods, public housing units, or other settings, such as public libraries or adult-oriented programming in public schools or community centers.

Forming resident committees, such as those established by the Los Angeles Human Right to Housing Collective, is a promising practice that adheres to both community organizing and human rights principles. Realizing "the right to adequate housing requires that individuals and communities are consulted and able actively to participate in the decisions that affect their right to housing" (UN Special Rapporteur on the Right to Adequate Housing, 2010, paragraph 77). As the Special Rapporteur noted, "a genuine consultation with, and participation by, all those affected, including the homeless, the inadequately housed and their representatives, should be guaranteed. Efforts should be made to ensure that residents are involved from the beginning of any redevelopment or other projects, and continue to be engaged during the entire process" (paragraph 77).

While social workers have addressed housing and homelessness as part of community practice, the profession has not addressed these issues as a primary focus. Housing, perhaps more than any other economic and social rights issue, is predicated on collective engagement. From a human rights perspective, fostering participation of those directly affected by the failure to ensure access to affordable housing is a critical element of community practice. As housing costs continue to rise in the United States and the supply of affordable housing contracts, the role for community practitioners in facilitating social action is pronounced. Yet, the lack of trained social workers familiar with the complexity of housing policy, in particular the failures of public programs to meet human rights standards, limits the profession's response. This chapter represents a framework for understanding housing concerns and policies through a human rights lens. We suggest that social workers take a leadership role in facilitating education and outreach on human rights principles to adequate housing.

Class Exercises and Additional Resources

For Discussion: Using the Findings of the United Nations Special Rapporteur on Adequate Housing in Advocacy

Raquel Rolnik, the Special Rapporteur on adequate housing, as a component of the right to an adequate standard of living, and on the right to non-discrimination in this context, visited the United States from October 22–November 8, 2009. The Special Rapporteur's visit focused on subsidized housing, homelessness, and the foreclosure crisis, examining in particular questions of affordability of housing, discrimination, and participation of low income residents in policy and program decisions affecting their lives.

Part I: Review the report of the Special Rapporteur at: http://www.ohchr.org/EN/Issues/Housing/Pages/CountryVisits.aspx (see link for 2010, 13th Session of the

Human Rights Council). As you read, consider which of the human rights concerns raised by the Special Rapporteur are relevant to your own community or practice. Does a human rights framework provide added insight or leverage to address housing within your community? Be prepared to discuss your ideas in small groups.

Part II: The Special Rapporteur made specific recommendations to foster meaningful participation of those whose housing was unstable, unsafe, or who did not have housing. These included:

- "Residents of public housing should have direct, active and effective participation in the planning and decision-making process affecting their access to housing. Residents should be seen as essential partners working alongside the Government in transforming public housing" (2010, paragraph 105).
- "The Government should create mechanisms to improve the participation of affected tenants in planning and decision-making processes. Residents' councils should be directly elected by residents and not appointed by housing agencies" (2010, paragraph 106).
- Public-private partnerships undertaking housing developments should include residents at all stages of planning, implementation, and decision-making" (2010, paragraph 107).

Consider each of the recommendations above and discuss in small groups the extent to which such standards for participation are already in place in your communities. How would you organize to facilitate such participation? What stakeholders would you engage and how?

Organizations Committed to Rights-Based Housing Mobilization in the United States

- Chicago Anti-Eviction Campaign: http://chicagoantieviction.org/
- Housing is a Human Right: http://housingisahumanright.org
- Moratorium NOW! Coalition to Stop Foreclosures, Evictions, and Utility Shutoffs: http://moratorium-mi.org/
- National Economic and Social Rights Initiative: http://www.nesri.org/
- National Law Center on Homelessness and Poverty: http://www.nlchp.org/
- Occupy Our Homes: http://occupyourhomes.org/
- OneDC: Organizing Neighborhood Equity: http://www.onedconline.org/
- Organizing for Occupation: http://www.o4onyc.org
- Picture the Homeless: http://www.picturethehomeless.org
- Take Back the Land: http://www.takebacktheland.org
- Urban Justice: http://www.urbanjustice.org/.

For Discussion: Criminalizing Homelessness and Human Rights Mobilization at the Community Level

The National Law Center on Homelessness and Poverty has identified the following as practices which criminalize homelessness and violate human rights. Review the list of laws and practices below and then consider the discussion questions in small groups.

- Enactment and enforcement of laws that make it illegal to sleep, sit, or store personal belongings in the public spaces of cities lacking sufficient shelter or affordable housing.
- Selective enforcement against homeless persons of seemingly neutral laws, such as loitering, jaywalking, or open container ordinances.
- Sweeps of city areas in which homeless persons live in order to drive them out of those areas, frequently resulting in the destruction of individuals' personal property, including important personal documents and medication.
- Enactment and enforcement of laws that punish people for begging or panhandling in order to move poor or homeless persons out of a city or downtown area.
- Enactment and enforcement of laws that restrict groups sharing food with homeless persons in public spaces.
- Enforcement of "quality of life" ordinances related to public activities and hygiene (e.g. public urination) when no public facilities are available to people without housing. (Excerpted from National Law Center on Homelessness and Poverty, 2011a, pp. 5–6).

Questions for Discussion

- Which of the laws and policies exist in your community?
- What is the rationale for their use?
- How are these laws/policies regarded by different groups (police, public health or social workers, religious leaders, public officials, business leaders, neighborhood residents)?
- Do representatives from homeless populations have an opportunity to respond to such policies and practices? Are their opinions taken into account in any meaningful way?
- As a community practitioner, how would you initiate a campaign to eliminate these practices and introduce local policies and programs that adhere to principles of the right to adequate housing?

For Discussion: Drafting a "Human Right to Housing" Report Card at the Community or State Levels

The National Law Center on Homelessness and Poverty is the leading national organization advancing a human rights claim to housing. Annually it produces a "human right to housing" report card in which it summarizes U.S. progress on implementing the seven elements of the right to housing. Consider the graphic below for use in public education or advocacy about the right to housing in your local community. How might this model of reporting be utilized at a community or state level to draw attention to the failures of housing policies to fulfill human rights obligations?

HUMAN RIGHT TO HOUSING REPORT CARD

Student: *United States of America*

CATEGORY	2011	2012	2013
Security of Tenure			
Renters	B-	C-	C
Homeowners	D+	D	D
Access to Counsel	D	F	D-
Emergency & Dire Circumstances			
Criminalization of Homelessness	F	D-	D
Domestic Violence	B-	C	A-
Availability of Services, Materials & Infrastructure	D	D	D
Affordability	D	D	F
Accessibility	C-	C-	C-
Habitability	C-	C-	D
Location	D	D	D
Cultural Adequacy	D	D	D
Overall	D+	D	D+

COMMENTS
Some progress, but needs more work!

The report card and an explanation of ratings can be found at: http://www.nlchp.org/HousingReport_2013%20copy.pdf

For more information on the National Law Center on Homelessness and Poverty visit: http://www.nlchp.org/.

Chapter 4
Building a Movement to Recognize Food Security as a Human Right in the United States

> *My husband thought about going to college, but it seemed like a nowhere situation in today's economy. So many of our friends are coming out of college and go right into the food stamp line because they can't get jobs. So my husband, a 4.0 student, decides against college and ends up a dishwasher. And we end up on food stamps. We're not "in the system" because we don't want to pay for our food or don't want to work. But it's a numbers game of being able to pay our bills and feed ourselves.*
> (International Human Rights Clinic, 2013, p. 7)

Introduction

In the past three decades, little progress has been made in reducing poverty in the United States, while various forms of inequality have increased. In fact, both have worsened since the onset of the "Great Recession" in 2007. A notable measure of increased economic hardship has been the growing use of food aid, such as the Supplemental Nutrition Assistance Program (SNAP) and the Special Supplemental Nutrition Program for Women, Infants and Children (WIC). Requests for private food assistance from religious groups and community food bank programs have also risen. Indeed, the ranks of the food insecure and those drawing upon federal aid almost tripled in the past 15 years. In 2001, nearly 17 million individuals received assistance under the federal Food Stamp Program (renamed Supplemental Nutrition Assistance Program in 2008). By 2009, approximately 32 million people used Food Stamps (Food Research and Action Center, n.d.). Beneficiaries of SNAP, the largest government food assistance program, receive on average $1.40 per meal per day, or approximately $4–5 per day. As noted below, such minimal assistance does not meet standards for the right to food, particularly in areas of the country where food costs are high.

In May 2013, the International Human Rights Clinic at New York University Law School drew attention to food insecurity and hunger as a pervasive human

K.R. Libal and S. Harding, *Human Rights-Based Community Practice in the United States*, SpringerBriefs in Rights-Based Approaches to Social Work, DOI 10.1007/978-3-319-08210-3_4 rights violation. The report on fulfilling the right to food in the United States, the first of its kind, asserts:

> The United States is facing a food security crisis: One in six Americans lives in a household that cannot afford adequate food. Of these 50 million individuals, nearly 17 million are children. Food insecurity has skyrocketed since the economic downturn, with an additional 14 million people classified as food insecure in 2011 than in 2007. (2013, p. 3)

Food insecurity exists when households report three or more food-specific negative conditions: they worry about running out of food due to lack of resources; the food supply runs out and there is no money to buy more; they are unable to afford food for balanced meals; adults felt they ate less food than they should; or adults reduced the size of their meal or skipped meals for three or more months (US Department of Agriculture as reported in Hoefer Curry (2012)). Reporting on the "new face of hunger" illustrates the reality of food insecurity and the difficult choices that Americans make daily. Testimony included in the International Human Rights Clinic report (2013) points to both resourcefulness and struggle faced by those who are food insecure. One young woman stated, "We've learned to be savvy with our food stamps. We use our food stamps on healthy food rather than buying cheaper, instant things or junk food. And plan ahead. Still, there are times when all we have left to eat is ramen. It's a little depressing, but at least we have ramen" (IHRC, 2013, p. 7).

The causes of food insecurity in the United States, one of the wealthiest countries in the world, are complex. Some communities are officially classified as "food deserts," because of the lack of access to locations to purchase adequate, quality food. In neighborhoods where grocery stores and other food outlets exist, prices may be so high that adequate food is not attainable, especially for millions of low-income families (Kaiser, 2013). And, throughout the United States, food assistance programs such as SNAP are unevenly administered, ridden with delays and challenges related to establishing and maintaining eligibility, while private food banks may not be accessible to the food insecure. Using a human rights lens puts the responsibility for action to promote food security squarely on the government. Without grassroots mobilization, however, the charitable and emergency-based response to address food insecurity and hunger will continue to fail millions of vulnerable individuals and groups.

US food assistance programs were created in the 1930s–1960s, when public support for such entitlements was considerable. However, growing political pressure now seeks to reduce spending and change eligibility standards to limit participation in federal food security programs (Hoefer & Curry, 2012). This retrogressive approach would be regarded as a human rights violation under international law, but in current political debates such goals are often portrayed as demonstrating "fiscal responsibility." Recent Congressional legislation has emphasized "out of control" spending on welfare, specifically the need to enact "Food Stamp Reform." Efforts to limit access to food assistance as part of a campaign to "downsize big government" have included state legislation calling for mandatory drug testing and work requirements of food assistance recipients. Since 1996, benefits have been denied to formerly convicted felons, under the guise of promoting personal responsibility. Public discourse on these issues has stressed the dangers of dependency on "welfare" and the unfairness of redistributing resources through government-funded food entitlements. This represents the antithesis of a human rights-based approach to adequate food for all on a basis of universality and equality (Davis & Dugger, 2012; IHCR, 2013).

What would a human rights-based approach to food justice mobilization and advocacy look like? How would human rights principles for practice differ from current approaches to food security in the United States? After summarizing international standards regarding the right to food and the parameters of US food policy, we describe examples of community-based practice to ensure a right to food in the United States.

Defining the Human Right to Adequate Food

The right to adequate food was first outlined in Article 25 of the Universal Declaration of Human Rights in 1948. It highlights the interdependence of social and economic rights, stating "Everyone has the right to a standard of living adequate for the health and well-being of himself and of his family, *including food* ..." (italics added). Additional protections were to be accorded to mothers and children. Securing food was thus embedded in the right to an adequate standard of living, and linked to housing, medical care, and the right to social protection in the event one could not work. The right to adequate food was given further legal substance in international law in its elaboration in the International Covenant on the Economic, Social, and Cultural Rights (ICESCR) passed by the UN General Assembly in 1966 (see Article 11 of the International Covenant on Economic, Social, and Cultural Rights (1966)). The UN Committee on Economic, Social, and Cultural Rights, which is charged with monitoring government compliance with international human rights standards, has established standards on the right to food. These are predicated on the principles of *accessibility*, *availability*, *adequacy*, and *acceptability* as core dimensions of the right to food (UN CESCR, 1999).

Food *accessibility* has both physical and economic dimensions. Individuals must be able to afford food (economic accessibility) for an adequate diet without compromising other basic needs such as housing, health care, or education. Food must be physically accessible to all people at all times, including those who may be physically disabled, the elderly, chronically ill, children, and others who are vulnerable within society. Access to food must also be guaranteed for those without direct access to food outlets (see Excerpt from the Committee on Economic, Social, and Cultural Rights General Comment on the Right to Adequate Food (Art. 11) (1999)).

In addition, food must be *available* to purchase in stores or people must be able to produce their own food (UN CESCR, 1999, paragraph 12). The UN Office of the High Commissioner for Human Rights (2010) underscores the link between poverty and violations of the right to food: "Often people living in poverty cannot fully enjoy the right to food because they cannot afford to buy adequate food nor the means to grow it themselves. However, the fact that they do not have the means to obtain food is also a result of persistent patterns of discrimination in access to education and information, political and social participation and access to justice" (p. 10).

International law underscores that *adequacy* of food cannot be interpreted narrowly, in terms of a "minimum package of calories, proteins and other specific nutrients" (UN CESCR, 1999, paragraph 6). Instead, *adequacy* should be determined "by prevailing social, economic, cultural, climatic, ecological and other conditions" (1999, paragraph 7). The Committee also stresses that availability of food must be "in a quantity and quality sufficient to satisfy the dietary needs of individuals, free from adverse substances, and acceptable within a given culture" (Emphasis added; UN CESCR, 1999, paragraph 8). Thus, adequacy must take into account each individual's dietary needs based on age, living conditions, health conditions, occupation, and sex/gender.

The cultural *acceptability* component of the right to food highlights the relational aspect of food. For a person to feel socially included within a given community or society, she or he should be able to access foods that are both culturally acceptable and desirable, as well as be able to gain such food through means that do not undermine one's dignity. The UN Special Rapporteur on the Right to Food underscores this principle, defining the right to include "sufficient food corresponding to the cultural traditions of the people to which the consumer belongs, and which ensure a physical and mental, individual and collective, fulfilling and dignified life free of fear" (UN Office of the High Commissioner for Human Rights, n.d.). So, for example, having to seek food at a local soup kitchen or to scavenge food from trash dumpsters to meet one's nutritional needs undermines an individual's send of social inclusion and dignity, thus violating not only the right to food, but also to participate within family and community life.

Critical to the notion of the right to food is that government is obligated to create an "enabling environment" in which individuals can secure food. The right to food puts the responsibility on governments to foster people's ability to "use their full potential to produce or procure adequate food for themselves and their families. To purchase food, a person needs adequate income: the right to food *requires States to ensure that wage policies or social safety nets* enable citizens to realize their right to adequate food" (emphasis added, Special Rapporteur on the Right to Food, Olivier de Shutter, retrieved from http://www.srfood.org/index.php/en/right-to-food). Ideally, all citizens and residents within a country would be able to purchase food with their own income and resources. But if not, governments are obliged to assure that social policies exist to address the rights of those who cannot work or whose income is not sufficient to secure adequate food.

In a 2012 investigation in Canada, the UN Special Rapporteur on the Right to Food found that realizing the right to food would require a food strategy grounded in a holistic approach which addressed developing rural economies, encouraged production and consumption of local foods, and the adoption of policies to improve food security and promote health (UN Special Rapporteur on the Right to Food, 2012). An integrated approach would need to address community development and policy making at a national and state or provincial level that integrated issues of "food, agriculture, health, transportation, economy and social protection" (2012, paragraphs 13–14). Of note, the Special Rapporteur stressed that while food policies which are more holistic are emerging at municipal levels, the benefits of such policies are unevenly experienced and must be combined with state/provincial and federal efforts to secure the right to adequate food for all. Thus, while specific locales may be mobilizing for food justice, a "national right to food strategy" must be developed to "effectively combat hunger, food insecurity and malnutrition" (2012, paragraph 15). While the recommendations of the Special Rapporteur were made to Canada, food systems and social policies, as well as the legal context about recognizing the right to food, are similar to the United States. Thus, his findings can also legitimately be applied to the US context.

Securing the right to adequate food is inextricably entwined with other human rights, such as the right to an adequate standard of living, to social protection, or to the right to housing. As the UN Committee on Social, Economic, and Cultural Rights finds, core principles such as governmental accountability (responsibility), transparency (openness), and local or community participation in setting policies, standards, and practices are crucial to securing the right to adequate food (UN CESCR, 1999, paragraph 23).

Until recently, the United States was one of the few countries to refuse to officially recognize a human right to food, illustrating the legacy of "American exceptionalism" with regard to international human rights standards and practices (Hertel & Libal, 2011). President Jimmy Carter signed the International Covenant on Economic, Social, and Cultural Rights (ICESCR) in 1977, signaling his intent that the United States would recognize economic and social rights as human rights. Yet, the US Senate has failed to bring the treaty to the floor of the Senate for ratification for more than 35 years.

Moreover, while the right to food was a rallying cry for advocates regarding US foreign policy in the 1970s, the government has distanced itself from recognizing the right to food that entail governmental obligations for provision in almost all official capacities. As Davis and Dugger (2012) note, "In international forums, the United States historically rejected the concept of a right to food and for years objected to any international document formally recognizing the right" (p. 204). In 2011, President Obama recognized a UN Human Rights Council resolution on the right to food. However, his administration illustrated its limited conception of this right by asserting that "everyone has a right to an adequate standard of living, including food" as defined by the Universal Declaration of Human Rights, but that it does not regard "the right to food as an *enforceable* obligation" (emphasis added, US Mission to Geneva, 2012). Despite formal US government rejection of this obligation, civic organizations at local, state, and national levels are engaging in rights-based discourses and practices regarding the right to food.

US Food Assistance Policy: Shifting the Focus to a Human Right to Food

The majority of public food aid in the United States is provided through the Supplemental Nutrition Assistance Program (SNAP, formerly known as Food Stamps), the National School Lunch Program, the School Breakfast Program, and the Special Supplemental Nutrition Program for Women, Infants, and Children (WIC) (Hoefer & Curry, 2012). These programs, while providing vital resources to people facing food insecurity, fall short of international standards on the right to food. Their eligibility requirements are often too narrow to include all who are food insecure; eligible participants face administrative barriers to participation; and benefits provided through the program are often not adequate to meet the food needs of recipients (IHRC, 2013).

Amidst rising hunger and food insecurity, advocates have called for increased food assistance, broader eligibility standards, and additional supports for the growing number of poor and working class people utilizing anti-hunger programs (Berg, 2008; Ratner, 2011; Weill, 2012). Yet, some of the most prominent food security activists have been reluctant to make a fundamental economic and social rights claim on this issue: that everyone is entitled to adequate food as a matter of human rights.[1] We argue that such a claim is vital: a human rights approach to food "shifts the focus from food assistance as charity to adequate food as a human right" (IHRC, 2013, p. 3). Access to the right to food is a nearly universally recognized norm that requires government to "ensure that all people have access to food that is safe and nutritious, meets their dietary needs, and is appropriate to their cultural backgrounds." In this view, reliance on emergency-based, charitable programs to address food insecurity represents an abdication of responsibility on the part of the government (Poppendieck, 1999).

Mobilizing Community Practice in Pursuit of Changing Food Systems

Community practice efforts related to hunger and food issues have lagged in comparison with the scale of food security concerns in the United States. The involvement of social work in these efforts has been especially uneven (Brown, 1988; Libal, Tomczak, Spath, & Harding, 2014). More than a decade ago, Biggerstaff, McGrath Morris, and Nichols-Casebolt (2002) claimed that "the social work profession directs little attention to the issues of hunger and food assistance programs" (p. 275). This assessment remains true today with a few exceptions

[1] An exception to this is the recent work by the NYU Law School's International Human Rights Clinic which released a report on the right to adequate food in the United States (IHCR, 2013).

(Hoefer & Curry, 2012; Kaiser, 2012). For example, the latest edition of *Social Work Speaks*, which showcases social policy statements adopted by the national office of the National Association of Social Workers, does not address food security and hunger (National Association of Social Workers, 2012). Thus, the impression is left that the US social work profession has little concern about food security, hunger, and food justice, despite the fact that social workers should be aware of the commonplace occurrence of food insecurity in most communities.

Community-based social workers could play a more substantial role in participating in rights-based organizing and practice to address food insecurity in urban, suburban, and rural communities across the United States. As Ife (2010) argues, "The importance of food, food security, the sharing of food … suggests that it can be an important focus for community, and as it also represents a fundamental human right it can be an important focus also for community-based human rights" (p. 195). Community-based work may help to reorient the social work profession to consider adequate food as fundamental to individual and family well-being. Taking a visible and collective stance as community-based social work practitioners could thus help to invigorate the profession's involvement on vital food security policy issues (Kaiser, 2013).

While entitlement supports, such as SNAP, are under attack in Congress, grassroots local food movements have emerged at a rapid pace. The "food movement" is multifaceted, with organizations, foundations, and community coalitions advocating for greater local, sustainable food production. These groups also challenge the dominance of agri-business and large food manufacturers in determining foods available for purchase. They also promote local and state efforts to make healthy, fresh foods affordable and available in urban locales. This emerging food justice movement seeks to "transform where, what, and how food is grown, produced, transported, accessed, and eaten" (Gottlieb & Joshi, 2010, p. 5). Though some urban food systems have been at least partially transformed, such as the approach pioneered by the Hartford Food System in the 1970s (Winne, 2008), these efforts have failed to adequately address growing rates of hunger and food insecurity (Nonini, 2013). And, while human rights-based approaches to housing and health have advanced in the United States, rights-based approaches to hunger and securing adequate food for all people have been rare (IHRC, 2013). As the following examples demonstrate, the right to food is predicated on grassroots mobilization and different forms of community practice. Social workers are thus well-positioned to work in collaboration with community members, in particular with families and individuals who experience food insecurity, to foster local capacity to realize the right to adequate food.

Rights-based practice for food justice entails organizing based on fundamental human rights principles of equity, universality, and participation (Rudiger, 2012). Of note, these concepts are aligned with social work values. At the core of the right to food is the assumption that individuals are able to provide for adequate food, housing, health care, and other basic needs through work (UN CESCR, 1999). When income is insufficient to secure food, housing, and health care, then government bears an obligation to either transform wage structures or develop other programs to fill the gap. For example, community practice that focuses on raising the minimum wage to a living wage may do as much as any policy or program to secure access to food. But community practitioners are also crucial conduits for organizing of information about inadequacies in the social safety net. Thus, they can also help challenge dominant assumptions that lack of adequate food is either the fault of those who are food insecure or that private charity can address human needs on an "emergency" basis.

Integrating the Cross-Cutting Principles into Community Practice

While few community organizations and social work community practitioners use a human right to food framework in the United States, movements are emerging in housing and health care that illustrate the relevance of integrating human rights into advocacy. These provide the opportunity for community practitioners to use human rights principles at the local level and in collaboration on campaigns at the state and national level.

Participation

Community practice is grounded in the notion of fostering community participation and power to effect positive social change through direct action, civic engagement, and collaboration with local officials (Rubin & Rubin, 2008). A range of tools and strategies can be used that build on a rights-based approach to community practice for food security. A critical first step is to involve local residents in assessing the root causes of food insecurity. Participation of community members is essential to identify local perceptions of access to adequate food and related concerns. Through processes such as a Community Food Assessment (Jacobson, 2007), practitioners can identify the extent to which the right to food has been realized in local communities, focusing on the dimensions of *adequacy*, *availability*, and *accessibility* (both physical and economic), and *acceptability*. In human rights terms, such assessment should be multi-dimensional, including efforts to gather the stories and testimonies of community members who struggle with food insecurity (Chilton, Rabinowich, Council, & Breaux, 2009). Analysis of available information through the US Census Bureau and other surveys can allow for compilation of data that reveals the systemic nature of food insecurity (e.g., percentage of children or elderly in a community who draw upon SNAP, WIC, or School Lunch or Breakfast Programs). Gathering evidence of human rights violations is only a first step. Community practitioners must also help to translate information about food insecurity, hunger, and poverty into documentation that can be used to pressure for policy change.

Some of the tools used by groups such as the Vermont Workers' Center to build support for universal health care are also appropriate to use in local and state campaigns to secure a right to food. Public testimony by individuals on their experiences of acquiring food and the ordinary, widespread experience of food insecurity can raise public awareness and pressure elected officials to move beyond "emergency" or "charitable" approaches to food insecurity and hunger. Bringing a variety of stakeholders together at public forums is essential to build powerful coalitions advocating for the right to food. Thus, low-income individuals, including vulnerable groups such as the elderly, unemployed, parents, those experiencing chronic illness or disability, must be joined by social workers, public health practitioners, public interest lawyers, religious leaders, teachers, school principals, those involved in food banking and community food system organizations, and advocacy groups.

The collection of testimonies, efforts to promote community dialogue, and evidence gathered of food insecurity can also serve a central role in efforts to use the legal system to create local change. In recent years, organizations such as the New York-based National Center for Law and Economic Justice (NCLEJ) have led a reform litigation campaign to address administrative failures to make entitlement programs such as SNAP accessible to all citizens and immigrants who qualify (Cohan & Mannix, 2012). Cases filed in Indiana, Connecticut, Hawaii, Texas, Colorado, Maryland, and New York have sought to address application delays that prevent qualified recipients from accessing SNAP benefits.[2]

Community practitioners also have a key role to play in public education about social and economic rights, the right to adequate food, and to promote broader knowledge of existing programs that address hunger and food insecurity. Such work is critical to fostering community participation to expand the scope of those who are aware of the existence of food systems programs, the deficiencies of these programs, and to craft more effective policy responses to ongoing food insecurity.

A recent example of community organizing for food justice is illustrative of the power of such an approach. Witnesses to Hunger is a program in Philadelphia that "seeks to advance social, economic, and cultural rights by increasing civic participation through a strategic public awareness campaign that is informed directly by low-income mothers of young children" (Chilton et al., 2009, p. 74). One effort by the group to amplify local women's perspectives on hunger and food insecurity in Philadelphia entailed using Photovoice, a participatory research method in which participants document their lives or a given issue through photography and telling their own stories. One aim of this technique was to "expose" public officials to the everyday realities of individuals and families who face food insecurity and hunger. Another goal is to raise "critical consciousness" of key social issues and to develop ideas about how to transform local communities and the broader society. In this

[2] See the NCLEJ's Web site for a listing of recent cases filed with partner organizations in these states. Information about filings and decisions is available at: http://www.nclej.org/key-issues-food-stamps.php.

project, it became apparent that women's understandings of nutrition and hunger were "inseparable from their experience of poverty and their access to welfare assistance programs" (2009, p. 77). Witnesses to Hunger created a Web site and, in collaboration with university colleagues and community practitioners, installed an exhibit of the women's photography in Philadelphia, Washington, DC, Boston, Massachusetts, and New Haven, Connecticut. Several women travelled with the exhibit and testified to the US Senate. The group also met with governmental agencies in Pennsylvania, specifically addressing problems they faced in "welfare to work" training programs, which in turn impact food insecurity among low-income households.

Researchers found that this initiative "promotes meaningful dialogue among low-income families, mothers of young children, the public, and policy makers regarding poverty, hunger, and the healthy development of young children" (Chilton et al., 2009, p. 76). Those involved in the Witnesses to Hunger project note that participation can be challenging, as low-income and minority groups "are often isolated from the American political process due to lack of adequate education, lack of access to technology, and structural disenfranchisement" (p. 79). These insights are similar to the ones discussed in the Foreword of this book concerning the importance of moving beyond tokenism to foster meaningful participation by low-income individuals and groups. The Special Rapporteur on Extreme Poverty and Human Rights argues that we must foster the right to "take part and exert influence in decision-making processes that affect one's life," noting that such action "is inextricably linked to the most fundamental understanding of being human and the purpose of rights: respect of dignity and the exercise of agency, autonomy and self-determination" (United Nations Special Rapporteur on Extreme Poverty and Human Rights, 2013, paragraph 17).

Transparency

The UN Special Rapporteur on Extreme Poverty and Human Rights stresses that "effective access to public information is a precondition for exercising other human rights" (2013, paragraph 60). The Rapporteur underscores that exercising the right to participation "depends on transparency and access to complete, up-to-date and comprehensible information." Thus, people must have the "capacity and opportunity to use the information, understand their entitlements and be able to evaluate the quality of the services, policies or programmes in question" (paragraph 60). In short, only through access to information can community members effectively engage in reform processes—participation—that assure the right to food. Information on the use of food assistance, disaggregated by indicators such as race and ethnicity, language use, household size and composition, and rate of labor force participation by those receiving food aids, is available through the US Census Bureau in its American Community Survey series.

While this data provides important insights into rates of participation in SNAP, other information is often needed to assess the degree to which local and state governments are implementing already existing food security programs. However, obtaining state-level data about processing times for SNAP and other benefits, potential racial disproportionality in the denial of benefits, or lack of follow-up by caseworkers on determining eligibility for food assistance is often a challenge. United Nations standards mandate that community organizers prepare and provide "appropriately designed information and tools" to individuals involved in social mobilization to realize human rights (UN Special Rapporteur on Extreme Poverty and Human Rights, 2013, paragraph 61). Fostering participation therefore entails using materials that are jargon-free and can overcome language barriers. Consideration of culturally appropriate means of outreach and dissemination of data must also occur, which could include communication in non-written form, via the radio, or disseminated through community meetings.

Accountability

Holding government accountable for failures in implementing existing food assistance policies is one way to advance the human right to food in the United States. Accountability mechanisms can be fostered through local commissions on food security, through human rights monitoring bodies which exist in many states, and through community-based efforts to investigate and publicize failures to adequately address food insecurity. Community practitioners and public interest lawyers have a potent role to play in pressing *state* governments to more effectively administer existing programs. For example, in 2012, advocates in Connecticut joined forces with a national legal aid campaign to sue the state Department of Social Services (Cohan & Mannix, 2012). The suit *Briggs v. Bremby*, currently under review by the United States District Court, charges the Commissioner of the Department of Social Services with "ongoing and persistent failure or refusal … to ensure the processing of food stamp applications in a timely manner, on a statewide basis …" This failure "has resulted and continues to result in the ongoing denial of food stamp benefits to thousands of households critically in need of this assistance to help them feed their families. Without prompt access to food stamps as mandated by federal law, these individuals face hunger and serious health risks" (*Briggs v. Bremby*, March 5, 2012).

The Connecticut case, part of a national impact litigation campaign (Cohan & Mannix, 2012), is premised on claims about failure of due process regarding access to social benefits. Should the plaintiff win the case, Connecticut's Department of Social Services would have to address organizational deficits that prevent the timely processing of emergency food assistance claims. The case will not result in a determination of a fundamental "right" to food benefits as a matter of governmental obligation, as there is no Constitutional recognition of such right. However, social mobilization at community, state, and national levels could press the US Congress to develop a national strategy for realizing the right to adequate food. Social workers—whether involved in community work, policy advocacy or clinical practice—can and should be central actors in this mobilization.

Conclusion

Community practitioners have been involved in mobilizing for stronger food systems, equity, access, and adequacy (for the right to food) for years, though their efforts were not often framed in these terms. Public health practitioners have been at the forefront of this work (Chilton et al., 2009; Chilton & Rose, 2009), while legal aid organizations and poverty lawyers have addressed a variety of barriers to participation in federal and state-sponsored food programs (Cohan & Mannix, 2012). These advocates have repeated the call to develop a national plan to end food insecurity and hunger, led by the government and informed by community members and various stakeholders (IHRC, 2013). As public health educators Chilton and Rose (2009) suggested: "Following the recommendations of the Committee on Economic, Social and Cultural Rights (General Comment 12), there should be a national strategy to implement the right to food. To implement the right to food means to put the structural processes in place whereby agencies, organizations, and citizens are working toward the common goal of actively respecting, protecting, and promoting the right to food" (p. 1207). The International Human Rights Clinic recently identified several policy steps that entail work at the national, state, and local levels to promote a right to adequate food. These recommendations include:

- Revise SNAP eligibility requirements to ensure access to all food insecure households;
- Increase SNAP benefits to meet minimum standards for a nutritious diet;
- Maintain SNAP as a federal entitlement program and shift WIC from a block grant program to an entitlement program;
- Develop strategies to increase children's participation in school meal programs (see also Poppendieck, 2011);
- Prioritize efforts to simplify processes for applying for food assistance benefits, to certify eligibility, and to continue verifying eligibility;
- Engage in systemic public education to raise public awareness of existing food assistance programs and reduce stigma from participating in food assistance programs. (IHRC, 2013).

As important as these steps would be in developing a national strategy, the plan would need to address broader, structural inequalities to have lasting impact. Beyond such efforts, systemic changes in job availability, wage and benefit levels, lack of affordable housing and effective public transportation, and the wider political economy of food production and consumption in the United States all shape food insecurity and thus must be a target of any national plan of action.

Following the insights of Biggerstaff et al. (2002), the social work profession needs to understand what forms of advocacy for food justice are occurring at local levels, as well as how to build effective campaigns to realize the right to food (Libal et al., 2014). The social work profession must also develop mechanisms through education, training, and consciousness-raising to better prepare practitioners to address food insecurity within their communities. Given the widespread and growing use of SNAP, WIC, the National School Lunch and School Breakfast Programs, and food banks for meeting basic food needs, the social work profession should be fully engaged in developing comprehensive food security programs. Integrating rights-based practices would reorient current approaches from charitable models, or blaming individuals, to an entitlement framework that emphasizes governmental obligations to assure that all those residing in the United States have a right to adequate food.

Class Exercises and Additional Resources

Article 11 of the International Covenant on Economic, Social, and Cultural Rights (1966)

1. The States Parties to the present Covenant recognize the right of everyone to an adequate standard of living for himself and his family, including adequate food, clothing, and housing, and to the continuous improvement of living conditions. The States Parties will take appropriate steps to ensure the realization of this right, recognizing to this effect the essential importance of international co-operation based on free consent.
2. The States Parties to the present Covenant, recognizing the fundamental right of everyone to be free from hunger, shall take, individually and through international co-operation, the measures, including specific programmes, which are needed:

    a. To improve methods of production, conservation and distribution of food by making full use of technical and scientific knowledge, by disseminating knowledge of the principles of nutrition and by developing or reforming agrarian systems in such a way as to achieve the most efficient development and utilization of natural resources;
    b. Taking into account the problems of both food-importing and food-exporting countries, to ensure an equitable distribution of world food supplies in relation to need.

Excerpt from the Committee on Economic, Social, and Cultural Rights General Comment on the Right to Adequate Food (Art. 11) (1999)

"The right to adequate food is realized when every man, woman and child, alone or in community with others, has physical and economic access at all times to adequate food or means for its procurement. The *right to adequate food* shall therefore not be interpreted in a narrow or restrictive sense which equates it with a minimum package of calories, proteins and other specific nutrients. The *right to adequate food* will have to be realized progressively. However, States have a core obligation to take the necessary action to mitigate and alleviate hunger as provided for in paragraph 2 of article 11, even in times of natural or other disasters …." (paragraph 6).

"*Accessibility* encompasses both economic and physical accessibility: Economic accessibility implies that personal or houschold financial costs associated with the acquisition of food for an adequate diet should be at a level such that the attainment and satisfaction of other basic needs are not threatened or compromised. Economic accessibility applies to any acquisition pattern or entitlement through which people procure their food and is a measure of the extent to which it is satisfactory for the enjoyment of the right to adequate food. Socially vulnerable groups such as landless persons and other particularly impoverished segments of the population may need attention through special programmes. Physical accessibility implies that adequate food must be accessible to everyone, including physically vulnerable individuals, such as infants and young children, elderly people, the physically disabled, the terminally ill and persons with persistent medical problems, including the mentally ill. Victims of natural disasters, people living in disaster-prone areas and other specially disadvantaged groups may need special attention and sometimes priority consideration with respect to accessibility of food. A particular vulnerability is that of many indigenous population groups whose access to their ancestral lands may be threatened" (paragraph 13).

Organizations Committed to Rights-Based Food Justice Mobilization in the United States

- Community Food and Justice Coalition—Oakland: http://cafoodjustice.org
- Food First (The Institute for Food and Development Policy): http://www.foodfirst.org
- Food Not Bombs: http://foodnotbombs.net
- Food Research and Action Center: http://frac.org
- Food Systems Network NYC: http://www.foodsystemsnyc.org
- Just Harvest: http://www.justharvest.org

- Los Angeles Food Policy Council: http://goodfoodla.org
- South Los Angeles Health and Human Rights Coalition: http://www.southlahealthandhumanrights.org
- Witnesses to Hunger (in collaboration with Drexel University's Center for Hunger-Free Communities): http://www.centerforhungerfreecommunities.org/our-projects/witnesses-hunger.

For Discussion: Making Connections: Developing an Advocacy Strategy for Right to Food Mobilization in the United States

Mobilizing communities and fostering a movement to challenge the dominant needs-based approach to food security in the United States requires creativity, vision, planning, and collaboration. This exercise encourages you to make connections between a documentary film on food insecurity and hunger in the United States and human rights principles on the right to food.

- View the documentary, *A Place at the Table* (Magnolia Pictures, Kristi Jacobsen & Lori Silverbush, Co-Directors, 2012);
- Review the UN Committee for Economic, Social, and Cultural Rights General Comment No. 12 on the Right to Adequate Food (1999); and
- Examine the recent human rights report, *Nourishing Change: Fulfilling the Right to Food in the United States* (IHRC, 2013) available at: http://chrgj.org/wp-content/uploads/2013/05/130527_Nourishing-Change.pdf.

Work in small groups to develop a strategy for advancing the right to food in the United States. Consider the following questions as you craft your strategic plan:

- Would you target your campaign at the local, state, or federal level, or all of these? What steps would you take in a 1–3 year period?
- What would you do to assess whether or not the right to food has been fulfilled (or has been violated)?
- Would you choose to address one aspect of existing food policy (like exclusions to federal food aid for those who test positive for substance abuse)? Would you develop a comprehensive campaign with a number of policy goals? What are the potential strengths and challenges of each approach?
- Who are the stakeholders you would involve in the process of developing a campaign? How would you do outreach? Foster participation (and with whom)?
- How would you frame the campaign? Would you use the language and concepts of human rights? Why or why not?
- What roles could and should social workers play in this campaign? How could you foster participation of a broad range of social workers?
- How would you work with advocates from other professions such as public health or law to advance your campaign?

Prepare a visual summary of your campaign and discussion points to share with the class.

For Discussion: Disaggregating Food Insecurity Data—Human Rights Implications

Research by Rank and Hirschl (2009) demonstrates that nearly 50 % of all children in the United States resided in households using Supplemental Nutrition Assistance Program (SNAP, formerly known as Food Stamps) benefits at some point during childhood. Moreover, they found significant racial disparities experienced by children, contrasting the fact that 89.9 % of Black children lived in households that used SNAP benefits at some point during childhood, compared to 37.3 % for White children (Rank & Hirschl, 2009).[3]

For Discussion

Review the International Convention on All Forms of Racial Discrimination and the International Covenant on Civil and Political Rights. Identify potential human rights principles that could be invoked to address high rates of childhood SNAP use as a means to secure adequate nutrition. What do you see as the strengths of invoking human rights in this case? What are the potential limitations of a human rights framework?

Rights-Based Activities Initiated by Communities

- Hold local or state hearings on food insecurity and hunger.
- Produce GIS mapping of community-level use of SNAP, WIC, and other food assistance programs.
- Conduct collaborative workshops with community members and community organizations on what the right to food means.
- Conduct a community assessment to understand why qualified consumers/beneficiaries do not access food security benefits and develop a local campaign to raise visibility about such programs and how to access them.
- Develop a short advocacy video through collaboration with youth involved in community gardens and/or outreach regarding food insecurity in urban locales.

[3] The sample size was too small for the researchers to disaggregate data allowing for comparison with Latino/Hispanic children (of any race).

- Apply a rights-based framework to review municipal and state programs for food security.
- Draft a shadow report for the review of the United States under the Human Rights Council's Universal Periodic Review (http://www.ohchr.org/EN/HRBodies/UPR/Pages/BasicFacts.aspx) or for the Committee on the Elimination of Racial Discrimination (http://www2.ohchr.org/english/bodies/cerd/), including gathering rights-based indicators related to food security.
- Coordinate with other groups to host the United Nations Special Rapporteur on the Right to Food (as has been done with rapporteurs on Extreme Poverty, Violence Against Women, and Housing) (http://www.srfood.org/en/special-rapporteur).

Chapter 5
Community Practice, Fostering Participation, and Human Rights

Dorothy Thomas, long-time human rights activist and lawyer, recently wrote about the challenges of fostering a rights-based approach to economic justice work in the United States.

> In the face of such entrenched inequality and the large scale of American denial that it even exists, adopting a human rights approach to U.S. economic justice work requires a profound degree of moral courage. The conviction that we are all born equal in dignity and rights not only prompts us to denounce abusive practices by extremely powerful actors, but also requires us to examine our own conduct. Are we, for example, constructing barriers between people that do not need to exist and do not reflect our values? The human rights frame encourages us to confront our own as well as others' biases and offers us a wider scope of possibility for novel forms of political solidarity, grounded in our common humanity, than those that are available within the narrower if more familiar framework of us versus them (Thomas, 2012, p. 350).

This book has urged community social workers to consider the consonance of social work values with human rights. It illustrates the potential of community-based social work to contribute to the realization of human rights in the United States. We focused on health care, housing, and food as human rights concerns that are central to contemporary social work practice, though they are more often framed as human needs rather than rights. We emphasized that making human rights claims requires having an in-depth understanding of international legal principles central to human rights (as well as an awareness of the status of US support for key human rights treaties). These include the following: respect for dignity, autonomy, and agency; non-discrimination and equality; transparency and access to information; accountability; and empowerment (United Nations Special Rapporteur on Extreme Poverty and Human Rights, 2013).

Efforts to realize human rights require grassroots mobilization and engaged community-level practice (Onazi, 2013; Tyler, 2013). As we have suggested, knowledge about human rights does not belong solely to lawyers, policy-makers, or other professionals groups; rather, it must also be fostered among the citizenry at large, especially those directly affected by key social problems. Community

K.R. Libal and S. Harding, *Human Rights-Based Community Practice in the United States*, SpringerBriefs in Rights-Based Approaches to Social Work,
DOI 10.1007/978-3-319-08210-3_5

practitioners can serve as important intermediaries between those who have typically been involved in human rights advocacy and monitoring—political elites and professional advocates—and the broader public. Indeed, in a country like the United States, which claims an "exceptional" stance by failing to recognize economic and social rights as human rights, community-based practice is a necessity. Social mobilization and participation of a broad group of stakeholders, especially those directly affected by the lack of human rights frameworks for health care, housing, and food, are needed to promote social justice and human rights claims. Without the judicial and legal means to enforce norms for the right to health care, housing, or food, community mobilization becomes a critical tool to foster policy change.

As we have shown, it is not easy to segregate distinct human rights issues; they are interdependent. Of note in recent years, civil rights advocates have begun to use broader human rights frameworks in their efforts (e.g., Lewis, 2011; Kaufman, 2011, 2013). Thus, some of the most visible human rights claim-making happening at local, state, and national levels concerns US obligations under several treaties it has ratified: the International Covenant on Civil and Political Rights (ICCPR) (United Nations, 1966a), the International Convention on the Elimination of All Forms of Racial Discrimination (ICERD) (United Nations, 1966b), and the Convention Against Torture and Other Cruel, Inhuman, or Degrading Treatment or Punishment (United Nations, 1984). In addition, advocacy at the Human Rights Council through the Universal Periodic Review Process has tackled a range of civil, political, economic, social, and cultural rights issues as interdependent concerns. Kaufman (2012) suggests that human rights lawyers and grassroots advocates have been able to address some aspects of economic and social rights through mechanisms to protect individuals against discrimination in the ICCPR and ICERD. US participation in these treaties "offers U.S. advocates opportunities to highlight ways in which ESC (economic, social, and cultural) rights are embedded within civil and political rights and raise a wide array of ESC concerns on the international stage" (2012, p. 412).

The approach used in this book to articulate human rights-based community practice for health care, housing, and food can also be used for other areas of community organizing. A few examples of vibrant local advocacy illustrate these points. These include community-based work to counter draconian "push out" policies for children and youth in schools who have been truant or have been suspended for minor behavioral issues (Bonazoli, 2012). The national Dignity in Schooling Campaign now uses an explicit human rights frame, pressing for the right to non-discrimination in schooling and the right to education (http://www.dignityinschools.org/). Another related concern is to address structural racism in the United States as it plays out in the "school to prison pipeline" and the phenomenon of mass incarceration (James & Smyth, 2014). Thus, momentum activists and organizers have begun to confront the related issues of differential sentencing and mass incarceration of persons of color as a new form of racism (Alexander, 2012; James & Smyth, 2014). The question of "over-representation" of people of color in the criminal justice system has been tackled at the United Nations through monitoring process progress under ICERD (UN Committee on the Elimination of Racial

Discrimination, 2008; United States Department of State, 2013) and at local levels (Human Rights Project of the Urban Justice Center, 2007). The effort to counter differential sentencing and mass incarceration of people of color is fundamentally a question of the human right to equality before the law, due process rights, and the right to non-discrimination. Similarly, the widespread and arbitrary arrests and detention of undocumented migrant workers are now being addressed as human rights matters central to local communities and social work practice (Androff & Tavassoli, 2012).

Throughout this book, we have argued that a human rights-based approach to community practice offers the potential to recast our understanding of issues such as access to health care, housing, and food as human rights rather than merely human needs. Such an approach can also foster active participation among those whose rights are not realized. As Thomas (2012) asserts, it can mean that those who are affected most by failures to secure economic and social rights can be "armed with the knowledge… to engage with those who would deny them those rights; and establishes a foundation of equality and respect that informs our expectations not only of the government but of one another" (p. 360). Community-based efforts to realize economic and social rights, some of which have been highlighted in this book, will continue to grow, and social workers have a central role to play in this movement.

Pathways for Community Involvement

Throughout the book, we have stressed a number of ways in which community-based human rights practice takes place. These actions can also be used in other human rights campaigns at a domestic level.

Community-Based Education

Carrying out human rights education at the community level is crucial to mobilizing diverse constituencies. Human rights education has long been fostered by the United Nations in countries around the world. Until recently in the United States such educational programs have tended to focus on civil and political rights. Experienced human rights educators note that successful human rights educational efforts at the community level "are designed with the knowledge that people tend to learn best what they feel they need to learn—information which is relevant to their own lives" (Human Rights Resource Center, n.d.). Effective community-based education "begins with soliciting information about the needs, issues of concern and experience of the learners. Many of the immediate concerns of communities and societies relate to economic and social issues." Community-based education can take place in community centers, through public programming offered by organizations working on advocacy related to housing, food, or health care; in faith-based organizations; or through collaborations between institutions of higher learning and community organizations.

Collect Testimony/Hold Public Hearings

Testifying and holding hearings about the failure to secure human rights is a common process for gathering insights into a given issue. Importantly, this practice can provide an opportunity for community members to express grievances, provide input regarding policy and law, and raise concerns about pressing issues within the community. Some states have established mechanisms to formalize this process, including Tennessee, where the Tennessee Human Rights Commission holds regional hearings and drafts an annual report on the "State of Human Rights in Tennessee" (http://www.state.tn.us/humanrights/). This effort brings together leaders from community organizations, government, advocacy groups, and researchers whose testimony contributes to the Commission reports that can be used in state-level advocacy. Community members can also testify before local human rights commissions, such as the Seattle Human Rights Commission, at regularly scheduled meetings (http://www.seattle.gov/humanrights/). In one innovation for the Universal Periodic Review in 2010, the U.S. Human Rights Network and WITNESS created the Testify! Project to facilitate creating video shorts of human rights testimony to be shared with UN representatives in Geneva. See information on the initiative and videos selected for submission at the United Nations at http://www.witness.org/campaigns/all-campaigns/us-human-rights-network.

Craft a Shadow Report on US Human Rights Record

These reports may be submitted for consideration by UN human rights committees that monitor the United States' progress on its human rights obligations for treaties it has ratified (Tars, 2009). An excellent resource to consult when planning to research and draft a shadow report is the website for the US Human Rights Network (see US Human Rights Network, n.d.). A powerful example of varied stakeholders engaging in human rights monitoring in the United States has been the civil society ("shadow") reporting process to end racial discrimination through the Committee on the Elimination Racial Discrimination (see http://www.ushrnetwork.org/icerd-project). The Universal Periodic Review before the Human Rights Council also offers an opportunity for civil society groups to highlight local human rights concerns (see http://www.ushrnetwork.org/our-work/project/upr-universal-periodic-review).

Participate in Community and State-Level Governance

Many communities have their own civil and/or human rights commissions (Kaufman, 2011). Community organizations can partner with such commissions, legal aid organizations, and other coalitions addressing food insecurity, housing, health care, children's rights, criminal justice, gender-based violence, immigrant rights, etc. Examples of efforts to implement human rights standards at a local level can be explored on the Web site for the US Human Rights Network (http://www.ushrnetwork.org/). Eugene, Oregon, for example, is seeking to implement social, economic, and cultural rights standards in the work of city government (see Eugene's Human Rights City Project at http://www.humanrightscity.com/).

Bring Human Rights Issues to the Attention of Human Rights Organizations

Social workers and community members can also report human rights concerns or violations to human rights organizations, spurring investigation and potential advocacy in partnership with such groups. Examples of partnerships to address human rights concerns in the United States are increasingly available online through the US Human Rights Network, the National Economic and Social Rights Initiative, the American Civil Liberties Union, Amnesty International USA, and Human Rights Watch. Formal human rights reports once drafted can be used in local, state, and national advocacy. For example, see Human Rights Watch reporting on a range of issues including the problem of homelessness faced by foster youth aging out of care (Human Rights Watch, 2010); the USA's "offender funded" probation industry (Human Rights Watch, 2014); and the criminalization of not paying rent in Arkansas (Human Rights Watch, 2013). These human rights reports not only document violations of rights, but they also provide useful advocacy steps and policy recommendations.

References

Albisa, C. (2011). Drawing lines in the sand: Building economic and social rights norms in the United States. In S. Hertel & K. Libal (Eds.), *Human rights in the United States: Beyond exceptionalism* (pp. 68–88). New York/London: Cambridge University Press.

Alexander, M. (2012). *The new Jim Crow: Mass incarceration in an age of colorblindness* (Rev. ed.). New York: New Press.

Alston, P. (2009). *Putting economic, social, and cultural rights back on the agenda of the United States*. Center for Human Rights and Global Justice Working Paper No. 22. Retrieved from http://www.chrgj.org/publications/docs/wp/Alston%20Spring%2009.pdf.

American Medical Association. (n.d.). *Professionalism and human rights*. Retrieved from http://www.ama-assn.org//ama/pub/physician-resources/medical-ethics/about-ethics-group/institute-ethics/research-projects/professionalism-human-rights.page.

Anderson, C. (2003). *Eyes off the prize: The United Nations and the African American struggle for human rights (1944–1955)*. New York: Cambridge University Press.

Androff, D. K. (2012). Adaptations of truth and reconciliation commissions in the North American context: Local examples of a global restorative justice intervention. *Advances in Social Work: Special Issue on Global Problems and Local Solutions, 13*(2), 408–419.

Androff, D. K., & Tavassoli, K. Y. (2012). Deaths in the desert: The human rights crisis on the U. S.-Mexico border. *Social Work, 57*(2), 165–173.

Armaline, W. T., Glasberg, D. S., & Purkayastha, B. (Eds.). (2011). *Human rights in our own backyard: Injustice and resistance in the United States*. Philadelphia, PA: University of Pennsylvania Press.

Austen, B. (2013, May 29). The death and life of Chicago. *New York Times*.

Barbera, R. (2014). Learning by doing: Integrating social and economic justice and human rights into social work practice in the United States. In K. Libal, S. M. Berthold, R. Thomas & L. M. Healy (Eds.), *Advancing human rights in social work education* (pp. 273–292). Washington, DC: Council on Social Work Education Press.

Becker, J. (2013). *Campaigning for justice: Human rights advocacy in practice*. Stanford, CA: Stanford University Press.

Berg, M. W. (2008). *All you can eat: How hungry is America?* New York: Seven Stories Press.

Berthold, S. M. (2015). *Human rights-based approaches to clinical social work*. New York, NY: Springer.

Biggerstaff, M. A., McGrath Morris, P., & Nichols-Casebolt, A. (2002). Living on the edge: Examination of people attending food pantries and soup kitchens. *Social Work, 47*, 267–277.

Biron, C. L. (2014, September 2). *Criminalisation of homelessness in the U.S. criticised by the United Nations*. Retrieved from http://www.ipsnews.net/2014/09/criminalisation-of-homelessness-in-u-s-criticised-by-united-nations/.

Bonastia, C. (2006). The historical trajectory of civil rights enforcement in health care. *Journal of Policy History, 18*(3), 362–386.

K.R. Libal and S. Harding, *Human Rights-Based Community Practice in the United States*, SpringerBriefs in Rights-Based Approaches to Social Work, DOI 10.1007/978-3-319-08210-3

Bonazoli, A. (2012). Human rights frames in grassroots organizing: CADRE and the effort to stop school pushout. *Northeastern Law Journal, 4*(2), 483–515.

Briggs v. Bremby. (2012, March 5). Retrieved from http://www.plainsite.org/dockets/s2lidj6w/connecticut-district-court/briggs-v-bremby/.

Brown, J. L. (1988). Guest editorial: Domestic hunger is no accident. *Social Work, 33*, 99–100.

Campaign to Restore National Housing Rights Blog. (2012a, May 11). *HUD Secretary Donovan denies community participation*. Retrieved from http://restorehousingrightscampaign.org/weblog/page/21/.

Campaign to Restore National Housing Rights Blog. (2012b, October 29). *UN Special Rapporteur on the right to adequate housing official visits New Orleans*. Retrieved from http://restorehousingrightscampaign.org/weblog/page/17/.

Carmalt, J. C., Zaidi, S., & Yamin, A. E. (2011). Entrenched inequity: Health care in the United States. In S. Hertel & K. Libal (Eds.), *Human rights in the United States: Beyond exceptionalism* (pp. 153–174). New York/London: Cambridge University Press.

Center on Budget and Policy Priorities. (2013a, January 25). *Policy basics: Federal Rental Assistance*. Retrieved from http://www.cbpp.org/files/PolicyBasics-housing-1-25-13RA.pdf.

Center on Budget and Policy Priorities. (2013b, January 25). *Policy basics: The Housing Choice Voucher Program*. Retrieved from http://www.cbpp.org/cms/?fa=view&id=279.

Center on Budget and Policy Priorities. (2013c, September 23). *5 things we learned from the Census about poverty, income, and health insurance*. Retrieved from http://www.offthechartsblog.org/5-things-we-learned-from-census-about-poverty-income-and-health-insurance/.

Center on Budget and Policy Priorities. (2013d, November 11). *Housing voucher utilization data: How to use the data*. Retrieved from http://www.cbpp.org/files/using-hvc-data.pdf.

Center on Budget and Policy Priorities. (n.d.). *Health basics*. Retrieved from http://www.cbpp.org/research/index.cfm?fa=topic&id=32.

Center for Economic and Social Rights. (2010). *United States of America: Fact sheet no. 11*. New York: Center for Economic and Social Rights.

CERD Working Group on Health and Environmental Health. (2008, January). *Unequal health outcomes in the United States: Racial and ethnic disparities in health care treatment and access, the role of social and environmental determinants of health, and the responsibility of the state*. A report to the U.N. Committee on the Elimination of Racial Discrimination. Retrieved from http://www.prrac.org/pdf/CERDhealthEnvironmentReport.pdf.

Chilton, M., & Rose, D. (2009). A rights-based approach to food insecurity in the United States. *American Journal of Public Health, 99*(7), 1203–1211.

Chilton, M., Rabinowich, J., Council, C., & Breaux, J. (2009). Witnesses to hunger: Participation through photovoice to ensure the right to food. *Health and Human Rights, 11*(1), 73–85.

Cohan, M., & Mannix, M. R. (2012). National Center for Law and Economic Justice's SNAP application delay litigation project. *Clearinghouse Review Journal of Poverty Law and Policy*, (September–October), 208–217.

Cox, R., & Pequet, J. (2012, December 4). Senate rejects United Nations treaty for disabled rights in a 61-38 vote. *The Hill*. Retrieved from http://thehill.com/policy/international/270831-senate-rejects-un-treaty-for-disabled-rights-in-vote.

CUNY School of Law and American Civil Liberties Union. (n.d.). *Youth incarcerated in adult prisons in the U.S.: List of issues nos. 13b, 16 and 18*. Retrieved from http://www.ushrnetwork.org/sites/ushrnetwork.org/files/19_page_262-270_youth_in_adult_prisons_intl_womens_hr_and_aclu.pdf.

Dahmann, N., & Dennison, B. (2013). Organizing for healthy communities: A report from public housing in Los Angeles. *Progress in Community Partnerships: Research, Education, and Action, 7*(1), 77–82.

Davis, M. F., & Dugger, A. (2012). A human rights-based approach to food security. *Clearinghouse Review Journal of Poverty Law and Policy*, (September–October), 202–207.

De Vos, P., De Ceukelaire, W., Malaise, G., Pérez, D., Lefèvre, P., & Van der Stuyft, P. (2009). Health through people's empowerment: A rights-based approach to participation. *Health and Human Rights: An International Journal, 11*(1), 23–35.

Deka, A. (2012). Local and global poverty: Insights from using a rights-based approach. *Advances in Social Work, 13*(2), 471–483.

Dewees, M., & Roche, S. E. (2001). Teaching about human rights in social work. *Journal of Teaching in Social Work, 21*(1/2), 137–155.

Finger, D., & Luft, R. E. (2011). No shelter: Disaster politics in Louisiana and the struggle for human rights. In S. Hertel & K. Libal (Eds.), *Human rights in the United States: Beyond exceptionalism* (pp. 291–312). New York/London: Cambridge University Press.

Fischer, W. (2013, November 22). *Rental assistance helps more than 300,000 veterans afford homes, but large unmet needs remain.* Retrieved from http://www.cbpp.org/files/11-7-13hous.pdf.

Fischer, W., & Sard, B. (2013). *Chart book: Federal housing spending is poorly matched to need. Tilt toward well-off homeowners leaves struggling low-income renters without help.* Retrieved from http://www.cbpp.org/cms/?fa=view&id=4067.

Food Research and Action Center. (n.d.). *SNAP/Food Stamp participation.* Retrieved from http://frac.org/reports-and-resources/snapfood-stamp-monthly-participation-data/.

Gable, L. (2011). The patient protection and affordable care act, public health, and the elusive target of human rights. *Journal of Law, Medicine, and Ethics, 39*(3), 40–354.

Gamble, D. N., & Weil, M. (2010). *Community practice skills: Local to global perspectives.* New York: Columbia University Press.

Gardiner, T. M., Irwin, A., & Peterson, C. W. (2009). No shelter from the storm: Reclaiming the right to housing and protecting the health of vulnerable communities in post-Katrina New Orleans. *Health and Human Rights Journal, 11*(2), 101–114.

Glendon, M. A. (2002). *A world made new: Eleanor Roosevelt and the universal declaration of human rights.* New York: Random House.

Global Finance. (n.d.). *The richest countries in the world.* New York: Author. Retrieved from http://www.gfmag.com/component/content/article/119-economic-data/12538-the-richest-countries-in-the-world.html#axzz306bMDqID.

Gomez, M., & Thiele, B. (2005). Housing rights are human rights. *ABA Human Rights, 32*, 2. Retrieved from http://www.americanbar.org/publications/human_rights_magazine_home/human_rights_vol32_2005/summer2005/hr_summer05_housing.html.

Goodhart, M. (2009). Introduction: Human rights in politics and practice. In M. Goodhart (Ed.), *Human rights: Politics and practice* (pp. 1–7). New York: Oxford University Press.

Goodnough, A. (2014, May 26). Hospitals look to health law, cutting charity. *New York Times.*

Gottlieb, R., & Joshi, A. (2010). *Food justice.* Cambridge, MA: Massachusetts Institute of Technology Press.

Healy, L. M. (2008). Exploring the history of social work as a human rights profession. *International Social Work, 51*(6), 735–748.

Hertel, S., & Libal, K. (Eds.). (2011). *Human rights in the United States: Beyond exceptionalism.* New York/London: Cambridge University Press.

Hertel, S., & Minkler, L. (2007). Economic rights: The terrain. In S. Hertel & L. Minkler (Eds.), *Economic rights: Conceptual, measurement, and policy issues* (pp. 1–35). New York: Cambridge University Press.

Hirsch, A. R. (1998). *Making the second ghetto: Race and housing in Chicago 1940–1960.* Chicago, IL: University of Chicago Press.

Hoefer, R., & Curry, C. (2012). Food security and social protection in the United States. *Journal of Policy Practice, 11*(1–2), 59–76.

Hoffman, B. (2012). *Health care for some: Rights and rationing in the United States since 1930* (Reprint ed.). Chicago, IL: University of Chicago Press.

Human Rights Project of the Urban Justice Center. (2007). *Race realities in New York City.* Retrieved from http://www.hrpujc.org/documents/RaceRealities_001.pdf.

Human Rights Resource Center. (n.d.). Chapter 5: Education and mobilization. In *Ripple in still water: Reflections by activists on local- and national-level work on economic, social, and cultural rights.* Minneapolis, MN: University of Minnesota. Retrieved from http://www1.umn.edu/humanrts/edumat/IHRIP/ripple/chapter5.html.

Human Rights Watch. (2010). *My so-called emancipation: From foster care to homelessness for California youth.* Retrieved from http://www.hrw.org/reports/2010/05/12/my-so-called-emancipation-0.

Human Rights Watch. (2013). *Pay the rent or face arrest: Abusive impacts of Arkansas's draconian eviction laws.* Retrieved from http://www.hrw.org/reports/2013/02/04/pay-rent-or-face-arrest.

Human Rights Watch. (2014). *Profiting from probation: America's "offender-funded" probation industry.* Retrieved from http://www.hrw.org/reports/2014/02/05/profiting-probation-0.

Hunt, P. H., & Backman, G. (2008). Health systems and the right to the highest attainable standard of health. *Health and Human Rights, 10*(1), 81–92.

Ife, J. (2006). Human rights beyond the "three generations". In E. Porter & B. Offord (Eds.), *Activating human rights* (pp. 29–45). New York: Peter Lang/Oxford.

Ife, J. (2008). *Human rights and social work: Towards rights-based practice* (Revised ed.). Cambridge, UK: Cambridge University Press.

Ife, J. (2010). *Human rights from below: Achieving rights through community development.* Melbourne, Australia: Cambridge University Press.

Ife, J. (2012). *Human rights and social work: Towards rights-based practice* (3rd ed.). Cambridge: Cambridge University Press.

Ife, J., & Fiske, L. (2006). Human rights and community work: Complementary theories and practices. *International Social Work, 49*(3), 297–308.

Inter-American Commission on Human Rights. (1948, May 2). American Declaration of the Rights and Duties of Man. Retrieved from http://www.refworld.org/docid/3ae6b3710.html.

International Federation of Social Workers and the International Association of Schools of Social Work. (2004). *Ethics in social work: Statement of principles.* Retrieved from http://www.ifsw.org.

International Human Rights Clinic (IHRC). (2013). *Nourishing change: Fulfilling the right to food in the United States.* New York: NYU School of Law.

International Human Rights Law Clinic University of Chicago Law, Chicago Legal Advocacy for Incarcerated Mothers, and American Civil Liberties Union. (2013). *The shackling of incarcerated pregnant women: A human rights violation commonly committed in the United States.* Retrieved from http://www.ushrnetwork.org/sites/ushrnetwork.org/files/17_page_229-254_shackling_uchicago_and_aclu.pdf.

International Women's Human Rights Clinic, CUNY Law (2009, November 30). *A gendered perspective on the right to housing in the United States: A report to the United Nations Special Rapporteur on Adequate Housing.* Retrieved from http://www1.cuny.edu/mu/law/files/2013/03/IWHR-Gendered-Housing-Perspective.pdf.

Jackson, K. T. (1985). *Crabgrass frontier: The suburbanization of the United States.* New York, NY: Oxford University Press.

Jacobson, M. (2007). Food matters: Community food assessments as a tool for change. *Journal of Community Practice, 15*(3), 37–55.

James, K., & Smyth, J. (2014). Deconstructing mass incarceration in the United States from a human rights lens: Implications for social work education and practice. In K. Libal, S. M. Berthold, R. Thomas & L. M. Healy (Eds.), *Advancing human rights in social work education* (pp. 413–434). Washington, DC: Council on Social Work Education Press.

Jewell, J. R., Collins, K. V., Gargotto, L., & Dishon, A. J. (2009). Building the unsettling force: Social workers and the struggle for human rights. *Journal of Community Practice, 17*(3), 309–322.

Joint Center for Housing Studies of Harvard University. (2013). *America's rental housing: Evolving markets and needs.* Cambridge, MA: President and Fellows of Harvard. Retrieved from http://www.jchs.harvard.edu/sites/jchs.harvard.edu/files/jchs_americas_rental_housing_2013_1_0.pdf.

Jones, T. (2011, December 2). *SNAP's homeless shelter deduction can provide much-needed help for homeless individuals and families.* Washington, DC: Center on Budget and Policy Priorities. Retrieved from http://www.cbpp.org/files/12-2-11pov.pdf.

Kaiser, M. L. (2012). Cultivating a landscape for food justice: An exploratory study of community food security measurement to inform community-based intervention strategies (Doctoral dissertation). Retrieved from *Dissertation Abstracts* (3530841).

Kaiser, M. L. (2013). Prioritizing health and community food security through the farm bill. *Social Work in Public Health, 28*(5), 509–519.

Kaiser Commission on the Medicaid and the Uninsured. (2013). *The cost of not expanding Medicaid.* Menlo Park, CA: Kaiser Family Foundation. Retrieved from http://kaiserfamilyfoundation.files.wordpress.com/2013/07/8457-the-cost-of-not-expanding-medicaid4.pdf.

Kaufman, R. (2011). State and local commissions as sites of domestic human rights implementation. In S. Hertel & K. Libal (Eds.), *Human rights in the United States: Beyond exceptionalism* (pp. 89–112). New York: Cambridge University Press.

Kaufman, R. (2013). Framing economic, social, and cultural rights at the U.N. *Northeastern University Law Journal, 4*(2), 407–417.

Leopold, J. (2014). *How homelessness continues to decline despite the affordable housing crisis.* Retrieved from http://blog.metrotrends.org/2014/01/homelessness-continues-decline-affordable-housing-crisis/.

Lewis, H. (2009). 'New' human rights? U.S. ambivalence toward the international economic and social rights framework. In C. Soohoo, C. Albisa & M. F. Davis (Eds.), *Bringing human rights home: A history of human rights in the United States* (Abridged ed.) (pp. 100–141). Philadelphia, PA: University of Pennsylvania Press.

Lewis, M. (2011). The human rights of children in conflict with the law: Lessons for the US human rights movement. In S. Hertel & K. Libal (Eds.), *Human rights in the United States: Beyond exceptionalism* (pp. 255–273). New York: Cambridge University Press.

Libal, K., & Hertel, S. (2011). Paradoxes and possibilities: Domestic human rights policy in context. In S. Hertel & K. Libal (Eds.), *Human rights in the United States: Beyond exceptionalism* (pp. 1–22). New York: Cambridge University Press.

Libal, K., Tomczak, S. M., Spath, R., & Harding, S. (2014). Hunger in a 'land of plenty': A renewed call for social work action. *Social Work, 59*(4), 366–369.

Los Angeles Human Right to Housing Collective. (n.d.). http://lahumanrighttohousing.blogspot.com/.

Lundy, C. (2011). *Social work, social justice, and human rights: A structural approach to practice* (2nd ed.). Toronto: University of Toronto Press.

Maciag, M. (2013, December 19). Cities where wages haven't kept pace with rising housing costs. *Governing.* Retrieved from http://www.governing.com/news/headlines/housing-cost-affordability-burden-increases-in-cities.html.

MacNaughton, G. (2011). Human rights frameworks, strategies, and tools for the poverty lawyer's toolbox. *Clearinghouse Review Journal of Poverty Law and Policy,* (January–February), 437–449.

MacNaughton, G. (2012). The human right to health care in the United States. *Clearinghouse Review Journal of Poverty Law and Policy,* (September–October), 208–216.

MacNaughton, G. (2013). Beyond a minimum threshhold: The right to social equality. In L. Minkler (Ed.), *The state of economic and social human rights: A global overview* (pp. 271–305). Cambridge, UK: Cambridge University Press.

MacNaughton, G., & McGill, M. (2013). Economic and social rights in the United States: Implementation without ratification. *Northeastern Law Journal, 4*(2), 365–406.

Massey, D. S., & Denton, N. A. (1993). *American apartheid: Segregation and the making of the underclass*. Cambridge, MA: Harvard University Press.

McGill, M. (2012). Human rights from the grassroots up: Vermont's campaign for universal health care. *Health and Human Rights: An International Journal, 14*(1), 106–118.

Mishra, R. (2005). Social rights as human rights: Globalizing social protection. *International Social Work, 48*(1), 9–20.

National Alliance to End Homelessness. (2009, October). *The HEARTH Act: Changes to HUD's homeless assistance programs*. Retrieved from http://www.housingalliancepa.org/sites/default/files/resources/177-HEARTH%20Act%20-%20PA%20Alliance.pdf.

National Association of Social Workers. (2008). *Code of ethics of the National Association of Social Workers*. Retrieved from http://www.socialworkers.org/pubs/code/code.asp.

National Association of Social Workers. (2012). *Social work speaks* (9th ed.). Washington, DC: NASW Press.

National Economic and Social Rights Initiative. (2010). *Toward economic and social rights in the United States: From market competition to public goods.* Joint Submission to the UN Human Rights Council for the Universal Periodic Review. Retrieved from http://www.nesri.org/sites/default/files/UPR_Report_NESRI_1.pdf.

National Economic and Social Rights Initiative. (2011). *Selling off public housing: A human rights analysis of HUD's new funding.* Retrieved from https://www.nesri.org/resources/selling-off-public-housing-a-human-rights-analysis-of-huds-new-funding-plan-march-2011-update.

National Economic and Social Rights Initiative. (n.d.). *Mayday New Orleans: Housing and Human Rights Organization realizing human rights in public housing.* Retrieved from https://www.nesri.org/programs/realizing-human-rights-in-public-housing.

National Federation of Independent Business v. Sebelius. (2012, June 28). Retrieved from http://www.supremecourt.gov/Search.aspx?FileName=/docketfiles/11-393.htm.

National Law Center on Homelessness and Poverty. (2011a). *Criminalizing crisis: The criminalization of homelessness in U.S. Cities.* Retrieved from http://www.nlchp.org/Criminalizing_Crisis.

National Law Center on Homelessness and Poverty. (2011b). *Housing rights for all: Promoting and defending housing rights in the United States* (5th ed.). Retrieved from http://www.nlchp.org/Human_Right_to_Housing_Manual.

National Law Center on Homelessness and Poverty. (2014a, July 3). *Racial discrimination in housing and homelessness in the United States: A report to the U.N. Committee on the Elimination of Racial Discrimination.* Retrieved from http://www.nlchp.org/documents/CERD_Housing_Report_2014.

National Law Center on Homelessness and Poverty. (2014b, September 22). *Criminalization of homelessness in the United States of America: A report to the U.N. Committee against torture.* Retrieved from http://www.nlchp.org/documents/CAT_Criminalization_Shadow_Report_2014.

National Law Center on Homelessness and Poverty. (n.d.-a). *Preventing domestic violence survivors from becoming homeless*. Retrieved from http://www.nlchp.org/prevention.

National Law Center on Homelessness and Poverty. (n.d.-b). *Preventing homelessness for renters*. Retrieved from http://www.nlchp.org/renters.

National Law Center on Homelessness and Poverty and The US Human Rights Network UPR Housing Working Group. (2014). *Housing and homelessness in the United States of America: Submission to the United Nations Universal Periodic Review, United States of America.* Retrieved from http://www.nlchp.org/documents/UPR_Housing_Report_2014.

Netting, F. E., Kettner, P. M., McMurtry, S. L., & Thomas, L. M. (2011). *Social work macro practice* (5th ed.). New York: Pearson.

Nonini, D. M. (2013). The local-food movement and the anthropology of global systems. *American Ethnologist, 40*(2), 267–275.

Nowak, M. (2005). The international covenants on civil and political rights and on economic, social and cultural rights. In R. K. M. Smith & C. van den Anker (Eds.), *The essentials of human rights* (pp. 193–196). London: Hodder Arnold.

Onazi, O. (2013). *Human rights from community: A rights-based approach to development*. Edinburgh: Edinburgh University Press.

Organisation for Economic Co-Operation and Development. (n.d.). *OECD health statistics 2013: Frequently requested data*. Retrieved from http://www.oecd.org/health/health-systems/oecdhealthdata2013-frequentlyrequesteddata.htm.

Organization of American States (1969, November 22). *American Convention on Human Rights: Pact of San Jose, Costa Rica*. Retrieved from http://www.refworld.org/docid/3ae6b36510.html.

Patient Protection and Affordable Care Act (2010). 42 U.S.C. § 18001.

Ploch, A. (2011). The long road to economic and social justice. In W. T. Armaline, D. S. Glasberg, & B. Purkayastha (Eds.), *Human rights in our own backyard: Injustice and resistance in the United States* (pp. 57–67). Philadelphia, PA: University of Pennsylvania Press.

Pollack, D., & Rosman, E. (2012). An introduction to treaties for international social workers. *International Social Work, 55*(3), 417–427.

Poppendieck, J. (1999). *Sweet charity?: Emergency food and the end of entitlement*. New York: Penguin Books.

Poppendieck, J. (2011). *Free for all: Fixing school food in America*. Berkeley, CA: University of California Press.

Pyles, L. (2006). Toward a post-Katrina framework: Social work as human rights and capabilities. *Journal of Comparative Social Welfare, 22*, 79–88.

Rank, M. L., & Hirschl, T. A. (2009). Estimating the risk of food stamp use and impoverishment during childhood. *Archives of Pediatrics and Adolescent Medicine, 163*(11), 994–999.

Rank, M. L., Hirschl, T. A., & Foster, K. (2014). *Chasing the American dream: Understanding what shapes our fortunes*. New York: Oxford University Press.

Ratner, L. (2011, December 14). Food Stamps: The safety net that deserves its name. *The Nation*. Retrieved from http://www.thenation.com/article/165169/food-stamps-safety-net-deserves-its-name.

Reichert, E. (2003). *Social work and human rights: A foundation for policy and practice*. New York, NY: Columbia University Press.

Reichert, E. (2006). *Understanding human rights: An exercise book*. Thousand Oaks, CA: Sage Publications Inc.

Reichert, E. (2011). *Social work and human rights: A foundation for policy and practice* (2nd ed.). New York: Columbia University Press.

Reisch, M., Ife, J., & Weil, M. O. (2009). In M. O. Weil, M. Reisch, & M. L. Ohmer (Eds.), *The handbook of community practice* (2nd ed.) (pp. 73–103). Thousand Oaks, CA: Sage Press.

Ross, M. (1955). *Community organization: Theory, principles, and practice*. New York: Harper and Row Publishers.

Rothman, J. (2007). MultiModes of intervention at the macro level. *Journal of Community Practice, 15*(4), 11–37.

Rubin, H. J., & Rubin, I. S. (2008). *Community organizing and development* (4th ed.). Boston: Pearson/Allyn and Bacon.

Rudiger, A. (2011). Reviving progressive activism: How a human rights movement won the country's first universal health care law. *New Politics*. Retrieved from http://newpol.org/content/reviving-progressive-activism-how-human-rights-movement-won-country%E2%80%99s-first-universal-health.

Rudiger, A. (2012). *Human rights and public goods: Why reliance on markets is bad for people's health*. PowerPoint presentation first given at the "Human Rights and Social Determinants of Health" Conference, Boston, MA: Northeastern University. Retrieved from http://www.nesri.org/resources/human-rights-and-public-goods.

Rudiger, A., & Meier B. M. (2010). A rights-based approach to health care reform. In E. Beracochea, H. Weinstein, & D. P. Evans (Eds.), *Rights-based approaches to public health* (pp. 69–86). New York: Springer.

Schimmel, N. (2013). The place of human rights in American efforts to expand and universalize healthcare. *Human Rights Review, 14*, 1–29.

Schott, L. (2010, July 13). *Using TANF emergency funds to help prevent and address family homelessness*. Retrieved from http://www.cbpp.org/cms/?fa=view&id=3234.

Segrue, T. J. (1996). *The origins of the urban crisis: Race and inequality in postwar Detroit*. Princeton, NJ: Princeton University Press.

Solomon, R. (2009). Global goes local: Integrating human rights principles into a county health care reform project. *Health and Human Rights: An International Journal, 11*(1), 105–112.

Solomon, J. (2013, October 4). *States' decisions not to expand Medicaid leaving low-income adults in a coverage gap*. Retrieved from http://www.offthechartsblog.org/states-decisions-not-to-expand-medicaid-leaving-low-income-adults-in-a-coverage-gap/.

Soohoo, C., & Goldberg, J. (2010). The full realization of our rights: Right to health in state constitutions. *Case Western Reserve Law Review, 60*(4), 997–1072.

Steen, J. A. (2006). The roots of human rights advocacy and a call to action. *Social Work, 51*(2), 101–105.

Steen, J. A., & Mathieson, S. (2005). Human rights education: Is social work behind the curve? *Journal of Teaching in Social Work, 25*(3/4), 143–156.

Swendiman, K. S. (2012). *Health care: Constitutional rights and legislative powers*. Retrieved from http://fas.org/sgp/crs/misc/R40846.pdf.

Tars, E. (2009). Who knows what lurks in the hearts of human rights violators? The shadow (reporter) knows—human rights shadow reporting: A strategic tool for domestic justice. *Clearinghouse Review, 475*(42), 476–478.

Tars, E. (2014, January 23). *Domestic human rights breakthrough*. Blog entry for National Law Center on Homelessness and Poverty. Retrieved from http://www.mdjustice.org/node/3835.

Terry, D. (2011, June 25). Foreclosed home is a risky move for homeless family. *New York Times*.

Thomas, D. Q. (2009). Against American supremacy: Rebuilding human rights culture in the United States. In C. Soohoo, C. Albisa & M. F. Davis (Eds.), *Bringing human rights home: A history of human rights in the United States* (Abridged ed.) (pp. 147–192). Philadelphia: University of Pennsylvania Press.

Thomas, D. Q. (2012). The 99% solution: Human rights and economic justice in the United States. *Northeastern University Law Journal, 4*(2), 347–363.

Tyler, E. T. (2013). "Small places close to home": Toward a health and human rights strategy for the US. *Health and Human Rights, 15*(2), 80–96.

United Nations. (1948, December 9). *Convention on the prevention and punishment of genocide*. Retrieved from http://www.ohchr.org/EN/ProfessionalInterest/Pages/CrimeOfGenocide.aspx.

United Nations. (1948, December 10). *Universal declaration of human rights*. G.A. Res. 217A, UN GAOR, 3rd Session, 1st plen. mtg., UN Doc A/810. Retrieved from http://www.un.org/en/documents/udhr/.

United Nations. (1951, July 28). *Convention relating to the status of refugees*. New York: United Nations. Retrieved from http://www.ohchr.org/EN/ProfessionalInterest/Pages/StatusOfRefugees.aspx.

United Nations. (1965, December 21). *International convention on the elimination of all forms of racial discrimination*. Retrieved from http://www.ohchr.org/Documents/ProfessionalInterest/cerd.pdf.

United Nations. (1966a, December 16). *International covenant on economic, social and cultural rights*. Retrieved from http://www2.ohchr.org/english/law/pdf/cescr.pdf.

United Nations. (1966b, December 16). *International covenant on civil and political rights*. Retrieved from http://www2.ohchr.org/english/law/pdf/ccpr.pdf.

United Nations. (1967, October 4). *Protocol relating to the status of refugees*. Retrieved from http://www.ohchr.org/EN/ProfessionalInterest/Pages/ProtocolStatusOfRefugees.aspx.

United Nations. (1979, December 18). *Convention on the elimination of all forms of discrimination against women*. Retrieved from http://www2.ohchr.org/english/law/cedaw.htm.

United Nations. (1984, December 10). *Convention against torture and other cruel, inhuman or degrading treatment or punishment*. Retrieved from http://www2.ohchr.org/english/law/pdf/cat.pdf.

United Nations. (1989, November 20). *Convention on the rights of the child.* Retrieved from http://www2.ohchr.org/english/law/pdf/crc.pdf.

United Nations. (1990, December 18). *International convention on the protection of the rights of all migrant workers and members of their families.* Retrieved from http://www2.ohchr.org/english/law/pdf/cmw.pdf.

United Nations. (2006a, December 13). *Convention on the rights of persons with disabilities.* Retrieved from http://www2.ohchr.org/english/law/pdf/disabilities-convention.pdf.

United Nations. (2006b, December 20). *International convention for the protection of all persons from enforced disappearance.* Retrieved from http://www2.ohchr.org/english/law/pdf/disappearance-convention.pdf.

United Nations. (n.d.). Quote from speech of Eleanor Roosevelt. *In our hands.* United Nations. Retrieved March 27, 1958, from http://www.un.org/en/globalissues/briefingpapers/humanrights/quotes.shtml.

United Nations Centre for Human Rights. (1994). *Human rights and social work.* Geneva: UN Centre for Human Rights (in collaboration with IASSW and IFSW). Retrieved from http://www.ohchr.org/documents/publications/training1en.pdf.

United Nations Commission on Human Rights. (2006, March 27). *Addendum to the report submitted by the independent expert on the question of human rights and extreme poverty. E/CN.4/2006/43/Add.1.* Mission to the United States of America. Retrieved October 24 to November 4, 2005, from http://www.refworld.org/docid/45377b5d0.html.

United Nations Committee on Economic, Social and Cultural Rights (CESCR). (1991, December 13). *General Comment No. 4: The right to adequate housing (Art. 11[1]).* Retrieved from http://www.unhchr.ch/tbs/doc.nsf/0/469f4d91a9378221c12563ed0053547e.

United Nations Committee on Economic, Social and Cultural Rights (CESCR). (1997, May 20). *General Comment No. 7: The right to adequate housing (Art. 11[1]): Forced evictions.* Retrieved December 13, 1991, from http://www.refworld.org/docid/47a70799d.html.

United Nations Committee on Economic, Social and Cultural Rights (CESCR). (1999, May 12). *General Comment No. 12: The right to adequate food (Art. 11 of the Covenant).* Retrieved from http://www.refworld.org/docid/4538838c11.html.

United Nations Committee on Economic, Social and Cultural Rights (CESCR). (2000, August 11). *General Comment No. 14: The right to the highest attainable standard of health (Art. 12 of the Covenant).* E/C. 12/2000/4. Retrieved from http://www.refworld.org/docid/4538838d0.html.

United Nations Committee on the Elimination of Racial Discrimination. (2008). *Concluding observations of the Committee on the Elimination of Racial Discrimination: United States of America, CERD/C/USA/CO/6.* Retrieved from http://www1.umn.edu/humanrts/CERD ConcludingComments2008.pdf.

United Nations Department of Economic and Social Affairs. (1995). *Copenhagen declaration on social development and programme of action for the world summit for social development.* Retrieved from http://www.un.org/esa/socdev/wssd/text-version/agreements/index.html.

United Nations Human Rights Committee. (1999, April 7). *Consideration of reports submitted by States parties under Article 40 of the Covenant Concluding observations of the Human Rights Committee Canada, CCPR/C/79/Add.105.* Retrieved from http://www.refworld.org/docid/3df378764.html.

United Nations Human Rights Committee. (2014, April 23). *Concluding observations on the fourth periodic report of the United States. CCPR/C/USA/CO/4.* Retrieved from http://tbinternet.ohchr.org/_layouts/treatybodyexternal/Download.aspx?symbolno=CCPR%2FC%2FUSA%2FCO%2F4.

United Nations Human Rights Council. (2010, January 4). *Report of the working group on the Universal Periodic Review: United States of America, A/HRC/16/11.* Retrieved from http://www.refworld.org/docid/4d6b6d3e2.html.

United Nations Office of the High Commissioner for Human Rights. (2010). *The right to adequate food, factsheet no. 34.* Retrieved from http://www.ohchr.org/Documents/Publications/FactSheet34en.pdf.

United Nations Office of the High Commissioner for Human Rights. (n.d.). *Special Rapporteur on the right to food*. Retrieved from http://www.ohchr.org/EN/issues/food/Pages/FoodIndex.aspx.

United Nations Special Rapporteur on the Right to Health. (2007, January 17). *Implementation of general assembly resolution 60/251 of 15 March 2006 entitled, "Human Rights Council," Report of the Special Rapporteur on the right of everyone to the enjoyment of the highest attainable standard of physical and mental health, Paul Hunt. A/HRC/4/28*. Retrieved from http://daccess-dds-ny.un.org/doc/UNDOC/GEN/G07/102/97/PDF/G0710297.pdf.

United Nations Special Rapporteur on the Right to Adequate Housing. (2010, February 12). *Report of the Special Rapporteur on adequate housing as a component of the right to an adequate standard of living, and on the right to non-discrimination in this context, Raquel Rolnik, Addendum Mission to the United States of America. A/HRC/13/20/Add.4*. Retrieved from http://www.ohchr.org/EN/Issues/Housing/Pages/CountryVisits.aspx.

United Nations Special Rapporteur on Extreme Poverty and Human Rights. (2013, March). *Report of the Special Rapporteur on extreme poverty and human rights, Magdalena Sepúlveda Carmona, A/HRC/23/36, 11*. Retrieved from http://www.ohchr.org/EN/Issues/Poverty/Pages/AnnualReports.aspx.

United Nations Special Rapporteur on the Right to Food (2012, December 24). *Report of the Special Rapporteur on the right to food. A/HRC/22/50/Add.1*. Olivier De Schutter, Addendum, Mission to Canada. Retrieved from http://www.srfood.org/images/stories/pdf/officialreports/20121224_canadafinal_en.pdf.

United States Census Bureau. (2012). *Income, poverty, and health insurance coverage in the United States: 2011*. Retrieved from http://www.census.gov/prod/2012pubs/p60-243.pdf.

United States Centers for Disease Control. (2013). Retrieved from http://www.cdc.gov/mmwr/pdf/other/su6203.pdf.

United States Department of Agriculture. (2013). *Supplemental nutrition assistance program: Number of persons participating*. Retrieved from http://www.fns.usda.gov/pd/29snapcurrpp.htm.

United States Department of Housing and Urban Development. (n.d.). *National Affordable Housing Act*. Retrieved from http://www.hud.gov/offices/adm/hudclips/acts/naha.cfm.

United States Department of State. (2010). *Report of the United States of America, submitted to the U.N. High Commissioner for Human Rights in conjunction with the Universal Periodic Review*. Retrieved from http://www.state.gov/documents/organization/146379.pdf.

United States Department of State. (2011, March 10). *U.S. response to UN Human Rights Council Working Group report*. Retrieved from www.state.gov/j/drl/upr/157986.htm.

United States Department of State. (2013, June 12). *Periodic report of the United States of America to the United Nations Committee on the Elimination of Racial Discrimination concerning the International convention on the elimination of all forms of racial discrimination*. Retrieved from http://www.state.gov/documents/organization/210817.pdf.

United States Human Rights Network. (n.d.). *How to write an effective shadow report*. Retrieved from http://www.ushrnetwork.org/resources-media/presentation-how-write-effective-shadow-report.

United States Interagency Council on Homelessness. (2010). *Opening doors: Federal strategic plan to prevent and end homelessness*. Retrieved from http://usich.gov/PDF/OpeningDoors_2010_FSPPreventEndHomeless.pdf.

United States Interagency Council on Homelessness. (n.d.). *Rights for people experiencing homelessness*. Retrieved from http://usich.gov/issue/human-rights/human-rights-article-2.

United States Mission to Geneva. (2012). *Explanation of the position by the United States of America, resolution: The right to food,* UN Human Rights Council, 19th Session. Retrieved from http://geneva.usmission.gov/2012/03/22/us-joins-consensus-on-hrc-resolution-on-the-right-to-food/.

Urban Institute. (2014). *How homelessness continues to decline despite the affordable housing crisis*. Retrieved from http://blog.metrotrends.org/2014/01/homelessness-continues-decline-affordable-housing-crisis/.

Venitis, P. M. (2011). Making human rights treaty law actionable in the United States: The case for universal implementing legislation. *Alabama Law Review, 63*(1), 99–160.

Vermont State Legislature. (2010). *Act No. 128: An act relating to health care financing and universal access to health care in Vermont.* Retrieved from http://www.leg.state.vt.us/docs/2010/Acts/ACT128.PDF.

Vermont Workers' Center. (2008). *Voices of the Vermont health care crisis: The human right to health care.* Retrieved from http://www.nesri.org/sites/default/files/Voices_of_the_Vermont_Healthcare_Crisis_2.pdf.

Weill, J. (2012). Food insecurity in America: A call to action. *Journal of Applied Research on Children: Informing Policy for Children at Risk, 3*(1), 1–9. Retrieved from http://digitalcommons.library.tmc.edu/cgi/viewcontent.cgi?article=1087&context=childrenatrisk.

Winne, M. (2008). *Closing the food gap: Resetting the table in a land of plenty.* Boston: Beacon Press.

Wolfe, B. (2012). Poverty and poor health: Can health care reform narrow the rich-poor gap? *Focus, 28*(2), 25–30.

Wolff, J. (2012). The human right to health. New York: W. W. Norton and Company

Woolf, S. H. & Aron, L. (Eds.). (2013). *U.S. health in international perspective: Shorter lives, poorer health.* Washington, DC: The National Academies Press. Retrieved from http://www.nap.edu/catalog.php?record_id=13497.

World Health Organisation. (2005 [1946]). *Constitution of the World Health Organisation.* Geneva: WHO. Retrieved from http://apps.who.int/gb/bd/PDF/bd47/EN/constitution-en.pdf.

World Health Organization. (2008, October). *The right to health.* Joint fact sheet WHO/OCHCR/323. Geneva: WHO. Retrieved from http://www.who.int/mediacentre/factsheets/fs323_en.pdf.

World Health Organization. (n.d.). *Backgrounder 3: Social determinants of health.* Retrieved from http://www.who.int/social_determinants/final_report/key_concepts_en.pdf.

Wronka, J. (2007). *Human rights and social justice: Social action and service in the helping and health professions.* Thousand Oaks, CA: Sage Press.

Yamin, A. E. (2005). Right to health under international law and its relevance to the United States. *American Journal of Public Health, 95*(7), 1156–1161.

Zaidalkilani, S. (2011). *Rights-based approach to community practice in Palestine: A case study.* Saarbrücken: VDM Verlag Dr. Müller GmbH & Co. KG.

32397037R00068

Made in the USA
Middletown, DE
04 June 2016